Marcia Nelson

Fiews buy ny

How to Raise Your Self-Esteem

OTHER BOOKS BY NATHANIEL BRANDEN

TO SEE WHAT I SEE AND KNOW WHAT I KNOW

HONORING THE SELF

"IF YOU COULD HEAR WHAT I CANNOT SAY"

WHAT LOVE ASKS OF US
  (formerly titled THE ROMANTIC LOVE QUESTION &
  ANSWER BOOK with Devers Branden)

THE PSYCHOLOGY OF ROMANTIC LOVE

A NATHANIEL BRANDEN ANTHOLOGY
  (includes *The Psychology of Self-Esteem, Breaking Free,* and
  The Disowned Self)

THE DISOWNED SELF

BREAKING FREE

THE PSYCHOLOGY OF SELF-ESTEEM

How to Raise Your Self-Esteem

Nathaniel Branden

BANTAM BOOKS
TORONTO • NEW YORK • LONDON • SYDNEY • AUCKLAND

HOW TO RAISE YOUR SELF-ESTEEM

A Bantam Book / March 1987

Book Design by Nicola Mazzella

Library of Congress Cataloging-in-Publication Data

Branden, Nathaniel.
How to raise your self-esteem.

    1. Self-confidence.   2. Self-respect.   I. Title.
BF575.S39B73   1987   158'.1   86-14644
ISBN 0-553-05185-7

Published simultaneously in the United States and Canada

PRINTED IN THE UNITED STATES OF AMERICA

RH   0 9 8 7 6 5 4

Contents

Acknowledgments

I wish to express my appreciation for the many helpful suggestions of my editor, Linda Raglan Cunningham.

I want to acknowledge my wife, Devers, not only for her invaluable editorial assistance but for her innovative work in the field of subpersonality psychology. She has contributed greatly to my understanding of the importance for self-esteem in integrating subselves. In this book, I deal only with the child-self and the teenage-self; in therapy we work also with an opposite gender-self—that is, a female component in males and a male component in females—and a mother-self, a father-self, an infant-self, and a higher self.

Preface

"It's not easy for me to be in love or to give love," says an attorney, "because in my heart I don't feel lovable."

"Whatever I do," says a college professor who is also a mother of three, "there is always a voice inside me saying, 'Not enough. I'm not enough.' There's not much joy in what I do, always trying to prove myself, just increasing exhaustion."

"What's the point of trying to accomplish anything?" asks an unhappy teenager. "I always feel as if everyone else knows something I don't know—and can't ever know. It's as if I were born missing something everyone else has."

"Happiness frightens me," says a man who has a drinking problem. "I have this sense that if I'm happy, something terrible will happen. So if things are going too well, I take a drink, and then another, and pretty soon things stop going well, but at least I'm not so scared—I'm in control, sort of—I know what to expect—I'm not waiting for lightning to strike."

"I know I sleep with too many men," says a woman twice married, twice divorced. "For a few minutes, when I'm being held, I feel that I matter to someone, that I have value. But that's self-deception and I know it. Afterward, I feel more alone, and I despise myself worse than before, which drives me to the next man. But how do I find a way out? How do I stop? How do I learn to love myself?"

How do we grow in self-esteem? How do we break the cycle of self-defeating behaviors generated by deficient self-esteem? These are the questions this book answers.

I began to see that such a book was needed when, while being interviewed following the publication of *Honoring the Self,* I heard a particular question again and again: "Dr. Branden, you have presented a comprehensive picture of the role of self-esteem in human life, and the devastation wrought by a poor self-concept, but in simple everyday terms, what can a person do, without the aid of a psychotherapist, to raise the level of his or her self-esteem? What can we do to believe in ourselves more, trust ourselves more, feel more confident about who we are?"

I saw that there was one more book on self-esteem I had to write. This book is not an extension of the theory of self-esteem, but *an amplification of its practice.* Its basic concern is with the *actions,* both mental and physical, that advance self-esteem or undermine it.

The strategies for building self-esteem that I recommend in the following pages have been thoroughly tested with thousands of clients in the three decades I have been practicing psychotherapy. On the more personal level, they also have been tested in the arena of my own ongoing pursuit of self-actualization. I have seen my self-esteem strengthen or weaken depending on the degree to which I consistently practiced the principles and practices this book advocates. I do not write as a detached observer, remote from the field of action, but as one who has lived that which I am writing about. These ideas *work.*

If your goal is growth in self-confidence and self-respect, this book is addressed to you.

However, because the book is action oriented, because it details specific exercises and behaviors in everyday life that raise self-esteem, it is addressed to professionals no less than to nonprofessionals. Psychotherapists know how badly our field needs specific procedures for transforming a poor self-concept. I hope they will choose to experiment in their own practices with the tools this book provides.

Chapter 1
The Importance of Self-Esteem

How we feel about ourselves crucially affects virtually every aspect of our experience, from the way we function at work, in love, in sex, to the way we operate as parents, to how high in life we are likely to rise. Our responses to events are shaped by who and what we think we are. The dramas of our lives are the reflections of our most private visions of ourselves. Thus, self-esteem is the key to success or failure.

It is also the key to understanding ourselves and others.

Apart from problems that are biological in origin, I cannot think of a single psychological difficulty—from anxiety and depression, to fear of intimacy or of success, to alcohol or drug abuse, to underachievement at school or at work, to spouse battering or child molestation, to sexual dysfunctions or emotional immaturity, to suicide or crimes of violence—that is not traceable to poor self-esteem. Of all the judgments we pass, none is as important as the one we pass on ourselves. Positive self-esteem is a cardinal requirement of a fulfilling life.

Let us understand what self-esteem is. It has two components: a feeling of personal competence and a feeling of personal worth. In other words, self-esteem is the sum of self-confidence and self-respect. It reflects your implicit judgment of your ability to cope with the challenges of your life (to understand and master your problems) and of your right to be happy (to respect and stand up for your interests and needs).

To have high self-esteem is to feel confidently appropriate to life, that is, competent and worthy in the sense just indicated. To have low self-esteem is to feel inappropriate to life; wrong, not about this issue or that, but *wrong as a person*. To have average self-esteem is to fluctuate between feeling appropriate and inappropriate, right and wrong as a person, and to manifest these inconsistencies in behavior—sometimes acting wisely, sometimes acting foolishly—thereby reinforcing the uncertainty.

The ability to develop a healthy self-confidence and self-respect is inherent in our natures, since our ability to think is the basic source of our competence, and the fact that we are alive is the basic source of our right to strive for happiness. Ideally, everyone should enjoy a high level of self-esteem, experiencing both intellectual self-trust and a strong sense that happiness is appropriate. Unfortunately, however, a great many people do not. Many people suffer from feelings of inadequacy, insecurity, self-doubt, guilt, and fear of full participation in life—a vague sense that "I am not enough." These feelings are not always readily recognized and acknowledged, but they are there.

In the process of growing up, and in the process of living itself, it is all too easy for us to become alienated from (or never to form) a positive self-concept. We may never reach a joyful vision of ourselves because of negative input from others, or because we have defaulted on our own honesty, integrity, responsibility, and self-assertiveness, or because we have judged our own actions with inadequate understanding and compassion.

However, self-esteem is always a matter of degree. I have never known anyone who was entirely lacking in positive self-esteem, nor have I known anyone who was incapable of growing in self-esteem.

To grow in self-esteem is to grow in the conviction that one is competent to live and worthy of happiness, and therefore to face life with greater confidence, benevolence, and optimism, which help us to reach our goals and experience fulfillment. To grow in self-esteem is to expand our capacity for happiness.

If we understand this, we can appreciate the fact that all of us have a stake in cultivating our self-esteem. It is not necessary to hate ourselves before we can learn to love ourselves more; we do not have to feel inferior in order to want to feel more confident. We do not have to be miserable to want to expand our capacity for joy.

The higher our self-esteem, the better equipped we are to cope with life's adversities; the more resilient we are, the more we resist pressure to succumb to despair or defeat.

The higher our self-esteem, the more likely we are to be creative in our work, which means the more successful we are likely to be.

The higher our self-esteem, the more ambitious we tend to be, not necessarily in a career or financial sense, but in terms of what we hope to experience in life—emotionally, creatively, and spiritually.

The higher our self-esteem, the more likely we are to form nourishing rather than destructive relationships, since like is drawn to like, health is attracted to health, and vitality and expansiveness are more appealing than empti-ness and exploitiveness.

The higher our self-esteem, the more inclined we are to treat others with respect, benevolence, and goodwill, since we do not perceive them as threats, do not feel as "strangers and afraid in a world [we] never made" (quoting A. E. Housman's poem), and since self-respect is the foundation of respect for others.

The higher our self-esteem, the more joy we experi-ence in the sheer fact of being, of waking up in the morning, of living inside our own bodies.

These are the rewards of self-confidence and self-respect.

In *Honoring the Self* I discuss in detail why such correlations exist. But I trust it is clear that if we wish to expand our positive possibilities, and thereby transform the quality of our existence, the art of nurturing our self-esteem is the place to begin.

Let us go still more deeply into the meaning of self-esteem.

Self-esteem, on whatever level, is an intimate experi-ence; it resides in the core of our being. It is what *I* think and feel about myself, not what someone else thinks or feels about me.

As children our self-confidence and self-respect can be nurtured or undermined by adults—according to whether we are respected, loved, valued, and encouraged to trust ourselves. But even in our early years our own choices and decisions play a crucial role in the level of self-esteem we ultimately develop. We are far from being merely passive receptacles of other people's views of us. And in any case, whatever our upbringing may have been, as adults the matter is in our own hands.

No one else can breathe for us, no one else can think

for us, no one else can thrust self-trust and self-love upon us.

I can be loved by my family, my mate, and my friends and yet not love myself. I can be admired by my associates and yet regard myself as worthless. I can project an image of assurance and poise that fools virtually everyone and yet secretly tremble with a sense of my inadequacy.

I can fulfill the expectations of others and yet fail my own; I can win every honor and yet feel I have accomplished nothing; I can be adored by millions and yet wake up each morning with a sickening sense of fradulence and emptiness.

To attain "success" without attaining positive self-esteem is to be condemned to feeling like an impostor anxiously awaiting exposure.

Just as the acclaim of others does not create our self-esteem, neither do knowledge, skill, material possessions, marriage, parenthood, charitable endeavors, sexual conquests, or face lifts. These things *can* sometimes make us feel better about ourselves temporarily, or more comfortable in particular situations; but comfort is not self-esteem.

The tragedy is that so many people look for self-confidence and self-respect everywhere except within themselves, and so they fail in their search. We shall see that positive self-esteem is best understood as a kind of *spiritual attainment*—that is, as a victory in the evolution of consciousness. When we begin to understand self-esteem in this way, as a condition of consciousness, we appreciate the foolishness of believing that if we can only manage to make a positive impression on others we will then enjoy positive self-regard. We will stop telling ourselves: If only I get one more promotion; if only I become a wife and mother; if only I am perceived to be a goood provider; if only I can afford a bigger car; if only I can write one more book, acquire one more company, one more lover, one more award, one more acknowledgment of my "selflessness"—then I will *really* feel at peace with myself. We will realize that since the quest is irrational, the longing will always be for "one more."

If self-esteem is the judgment that I am appropriate to life, the experience of competence and worth—if self-esteem is self-affirming consciousness, a mind that trusts itself—no one can generate this experience except myself.

When we appreciate the true nature of self-esteem, we see that it is not competitive or comparative.

Genuine self-esteem is not expressed by self-glorification at the expense of others, or by the quest to make oneself superior to others or to diminish others so as to elevate oneself. Arrogance, boastfulness, and the overestimation of our abilities reflect inadequate self-esteem rather than, as some people imagine, too much self-esteem.

One of the most significant characteristics of healthy self-esteem is that it is *the state of one who is not at war either with himself or with others.*

The importance of healthy self-esteem lies in the fact that it is the foundation of our ability to respond actively and positively to the opportunities of life—in work, in love, and in play. It is also the foundation of that serenity of spirit that makes possible the enjoyment of life.

Chapter 2
Self-Concept As Destiny

Our *self-concept* is who and what we consciously and subconsciously think we are—our physical and psychological traits, our assets and liabilities, and, above all, our self-esteem. Self-esteem is the *evaluative* component of self-concept.

Our self-concept shapes our destiny; that is, our deepest vision of ourselves influences all of our significant choices and decisions and therefore shapes the kind of life we create for ourselves.

The following brief illustrations are offered to clarify how our self-concept affects our feelings and behavior. Read the stories with that perspective in mind.

Jane was a thirty-four-year-old saleswoman in a large department store. Although she was in a relationship with a man she described as "comfortable," she had never married. At our first meeting she explained that she did not have a specific complaint so much as a general sense of dissatisfaction, a feeling that "there must be more to life than this." Then she added, "I'd like to understand myself better and I'd like to learn to be more self-assertive."

I asked her to close her eyes and enter the following fantasy:

"Imagine you are standing at the foot of a mountain, any kind of mountain you wish to create. There is a footpath leading up to the very top. You begin to walk. You feel the pull on your leg muscles as you climb. Are there trees and flowers on the side of this mountain? . . . As you climb, you become aware of something very interesting. All the fears and doubts and insecurities of your everyday life seem to fall away, like so much excess baggage you no longer need. The higher you climb, the freer you feel. As you approach the top of the mountain, notice that you feel almost weightless. Your mind is clear. You feel stronger, more sure of yourself than you have ever felt in your life. Imagine this state and explore it. Do you like it? And how does your body feel when you are self-confident and free of doubt and fear? . . . And now you are just a few steps from the very top of the mountain. Now you stand on the top, looking out over the world. How do you feel? What is your sense of your relationship to the world now? What is it like to be without the old familiar insecurities? Take a few minutes to explore that. . . . And now turn and begin your descent back down the mountain. And as you follow the footpath down, notice whether you bring your new strength and freedom with you or whether you leave those feelings at the top of the mountain. Do the old weights return as you approach the bottom? And as you come back to the point at which you started, can you look at the world from a new perspective? How do you feel? What changes? Do you experience yourself differently?"

After a few moments she opened her eyes. "I loved it at the top. I felt like myself, yet it's a self I've never been. And I was lonely. And frightened. And I heard my mother's voice saying, 'You don't belong here.' As I was coming back down the mountain, I felt the old heaviness returning, but not entirely. Something felt different. And there was one moment up there when . . . when I was free. Really free. I knew I could do anything. Knew nothing was stopping me, except me. I could really feel that, experience it, not as some kind of theory, you know, but something real, something I felt in my body and saw with my whole mind. Almost like a moment of intoxication. Except that this intoxication didn't blind me to reality. It was more like a gaining of sight."

"But," I suggested, "to rise higher might mean to go against your mother? To contradict her view of things?"

"I suppose . . . not to be her daughter anymore."

"And, looked at that way, it feels like a hard choice."

"Can I like myself if my mother doesn't?"

"Can you?" I prompted.

"I don't see why not. And maybe she'll learn to. Maybe she'll adjust to me rather than me to her."

"Have you ever thought about the fact that just about every version of the hero's journey starts with the hero leaving home, cutting loose of the gravitational pull of family?"

The focus of my work with Jane was on teaching her greater self-awareness (awareness of feelings, desires, thoughts, and abilities), self-acceptance (learning not to disown her experience or be in an adversarial relationship with herself), and self-expression in action (self-assertion), which are among the most important pillars of self-esteem. Jane used the vision of embarking on a journey to help her break her family ties; it gave her a new perspective. After several months in therapy she said she had achieved her goal, and therapy was terminated.

Six months later I received a cheerful letter in which

she reported that a week after leaving therapy she had quit her job to start her own retail business, "something I had wanted to do for years but hadn't the nerve," and her store was now prospering. "In our family, women weren't supposed to have a head for business, but I'm through with all that foolishness now. What I got from therapy is that my life belongs to me—isn't that basic to self-esteem?—and that if there's something I really want, why shouldn't I go after it? Now I'm ready to start thinking about relationships."

Jane was not without self-esteem when she first consulted me. However, some part of her self-esteem had been invested in false values: in the belief that her mother's approval was necessary to her well-being and her self-respect. In learning to withdraw that investment, to take her life back into her own hands and to live by her own judgment, she raised her self-esteem naturally and opened the door to possibilities that previously she had felt were beyond her reach.

Does any aspect of Jane's story relate to your experience?

Charles, a fifty-year-old, highly successful investment banker, came to see me because of profound unhappiness with his personal relationships and a deep-rooted fear that was masked by an appearance of calmness and self-assurance. "It's unbelievably easy to fool people about my self-confidence," he said. "That's because they're insecure too." Divorced after fifteen years of marriage, he had been with the same woman for the past three years, breaking up and reuniting and breaking up again. "The simple truth is that I don't have a lot of regard for her. But she adores me, she clings to me, she wants to be with me all the time. It's safe and simple. We fight because I don't want to get married. I put her down, I reproach her for past affairs. She screams that I'm afraid of commitment. Why should I want to commit to a woman who really, deep down, doesn't interest me? So what am I doing with her?"

What I saw when I looked into the face of this middle-aged man with thinning hair was a young boy who was frightened, bewildered, anguished, and seemed to be reaching out for help from the depths of some nightmare of his past. I was perfectly willing to believe that was not how his associates saw him, but I wondered how they could escape seeing it. And I thought that his sense of invisibility could only be adding to his torment.

The only child of impoverished Russian immigrants, he had been raised, he said, without love, without the slightest hint of warmth or affection, and with a good deal of humiliating physical brutality. "But I knew I was smart and I knew I could survive. I knew I could see things other people couldn't—like how to make money. I was running my first successful business when I was fourteen. I wanted money so I could be free. Today I make a great deal. Operating in business is easy for me. I don't know why, but it is. The right moves just seem obvious. In terms of my personal life, I tried a couple of times to confide in one of my partners about my insecurities. He laughed at me, wouldn't believe me, didn't even want to hear about it. I live in a two-room apartment and have no interest in personal amenities. I feel I don't deserve them. I feel I hardly deserve anything. . . . You know what I like about you? You see my fear and my pain and you believe it, you're not afraid of it, you don't try to change the subject."

"And speaking of that," I said, "I wonder what it was like to be a five-year-old boy living in your house."

Tears came to his eyes as he told me the ways in which it had been truly terrible. As he spoke, the child he once had been emerged more and more clearly in his face.

It was apparent that as a child, notwithstanding his ferocious will to survive, Charles had formed an appallingly low self-concept, which accounted both for his feeling of being undeserving and for his choice of a woman whom he held in low esteem. Who was he to have the love of an admirable woman? And while he allowed himself to make money, he did not allow himself to enjoy it.

I decided that the child—or, more precisely, the child-self within the adult—held the key to reclaiming Charles's self-esteem. Since the concept of a child-self is important and will appear again later in the book, let us pause to understand it.

Each of us was once a child, and, although we may not realize it, we carry that child within us, as an aspect of who we are. Sometimes we shift into the state of consciousness of the child we once were, and respond to situations in our adult lives as if, for all practical purposes, we were still that child, with his or her values, emotions, perspectives, and distinctive way of processing experience. Sometimes this is desirable—for example, when we experience the child's spontaneity and playfulness. It is undesirable, however, when we reactivate that child's insecurities, dependency, and limited grasp of the world.

We can learn to recognize that child, make friends with him or her, and listen attentively to what the child needs to tell us, even if it is painful. We can allow the child, in effect, to feel welcome within us, thereby allowing the child-self to be integrated into our adult-self. Or we can disown the child, out of fear, pain, or embarrassment, making ourselves unconscious of his or her existence and needs. In the latter case, the child-self, left abandoned and unintegrated, typically proceeds to wreak havoc in our lives in ways that we are unlikely to recognize: making it impossible for us to have a happy love life, leading us to inappropriate behaviors at work, denying us the freedom of adult forms of play, and so forth.

I wanted to explore the hypothesis that Charles's early years had been so painful that he had psychologically numbed himself in order to survive, that in the process of maturing he had left his child-self in an airtight chamber where his screams could barely be heard, and that the redemption of his self-esteem could not begin until he had redeemed that child-self. With his child-self feeling rejected and repudiated by his adult-self, with one part of him so ruthlessly condemned by another part, there was no way for his self-esteem to survive unimpaired.

The early stages of therapy, therefore, concentrated on guiding Charles through his childhood years, allowing him to experience at deeper and deeper levels the indignities, humiliations, and overall sense of danger and chaos that had formed his first impressions of life. This was accomplished principally through a sentence-completion procedure that figures prominently in my method of therapy. I explained to Charles that I would give him a sentence stem, an incomplete sentence, and he would keep repeating that stem, finishing the sentence with a different ending each time, without worrying if every ending was literally true or if one ending seemed to conflict with another. Following are some excerpts from our early therapy sessions.

I gave him the stem **If the child within could speak, he would say**— and here are his endings:

I'm afraid.
I don't understand.
why is Mother always shouting at me?
why is Father hitting me?
why does nothing make sense?
why won't anyone play with me?
I don't know how to talk to anyone.
I have nightmares all the time, and when I cry Daddy screams at me.
when I'm taking a bath, why does Daddy come in and make fun of me?
why does no one protect me?

Then I gave him the stem **One of the things I had to do to survive was**—

to be cautious.
not feel.
hide.
read.
keep my eyes open every minute.
always be alert for danger.
trust no one.
learn to be independent.

Then, in a later session: **One of the things my child-self needs from me is**—

permission to be spontaneous.
to listen.
to make him feel safe.
to let him cry.
to hold him.
not to punish him as Father did.

to hear his pain.
to comfort him.
to be there.
not to run away from him.

If I were to be more compassionate and loving toward my child-self—

I would let him play more.
he would feel less alone.
he wouldn't feel abandoned by everyone.
I could be the father he never had.
I'd let him enjoy things.
I could make the world right for him.
he could feel safe.
we both could feel safe.
I could heal him and heal myself.

When we had explored these themes in some detail, I said to Charles, "Could you close your eyes, please, and imagine little Charles standing in front of you. And how is he looking at you? What is the expression in his eyes? And I wonder how you would feel, right now, if you were to reach out and lift him onto your lap and just hold him, and let your arms tell him that he's safe, that you're there now, and that you'll always be there, that he can rely on and trust someone at last."

I wanted Charles to experience his child-self as a separate entity, while simultaneously retaining the knowledge that he was dealing with a disowned aspect of himself, which subsequently he would have to integrate.

Charles began to weep softly. "He looks hurt, and angry, and distrustful, and wanting so much to trust. . . . This feels so good," he whispered.

"That's right . . . and allow him to weep with you . . . the two of you weeping together . . . really understanding things now . . . so much more than can be put into words . . . words are not necessary . . . and you can feel that. . . ."

Through imagination and guided fantasy, Charles reached back in time to rescue his child-self, to defuse his pain, and to provide the comfort, support, and consistency that the child had never known. In so doing, Charles began to "forgive" that child, to "forgive" his child-self— *to understand that no forgiveness was necessary*—for the fact that the child had not known how to cope any better than he did, *the child was struggling to survive the only way he knew* . . . and as this perspective became absorbed and integrated, Charles's self-esteem began to climb.

And as his self-esteem grew stronger, Charles began to appear at once more adult and more masculine. His child-self added life to his face rather than pain. In the following weeks he instituted more changes in his life, entirely on his own initiative. He began to dress better, no longer ashamed that he could afford expensive clothes. He moved from his modest apartment to an attractive home. He ended his unsatisfying three-year relationship and began dating women of higher intelligence, achievement, and independence. He projected more energy and decisiveness. He looked more alive.

In reclaiming and integrating an important but *disowned* part of himself, he grew in stature in his own eyes. In transforming his self-esteem, he transformed his life.

I suggest you take a moment to explore your feelings toward the child you once were, and to wonder about the role your child-self might occupy in your life today.

* * *

Eva, age fifteen, was failing in school. She rarely came home from school or dates at the time she had promised. Her parents complained of her frequent lies. Her mother, who confided that her own life had been rather "wild" prior to her marriage, said to me, "I'm terrified. Eva is so much like me at her age." Eva's father, a stockbroker, confided, "I was a teenager and I know what can go on. I wasn't an angel myself, as Eva well knows, as she's heard her mother and me talk about it. I love Eva and I'm concerned about her behavior."

Eva's older brother was a good student and a model son. In therapy Eva admitted that she perceived him as the better-looking and more intelligent of the two. She knew she was quick to provoke quarrels with him. It very quickly became evident to me that the only way Eva knew to gain attention was to be "bad." In other words, she had a poor self-concept and seemed intent on translating it into an unhappy life. The question was: how to generate a change in self-concept and in behavior?

I asked her to sit in front of a mirror and study herself. She said she intensely disliked doing so; she saw everything she disliked in herself reflected in the mirror.

I suggested that if she could go a whole week without telling anyone a single lie, she would be surprised at the change she would notice in the mirror at our next session, although the change would probably be subtle and she would have to have very keen eyes to observe it. She thought this was silly but agreed to do the assignment. I separately asked her parents to accept anything she said that week and not to challenge her truthfulness.

At our next session she sat in front of the mirror and said, "I look worse." Then she confessed that she had told her mother three lies. She was astonished that she had not been called on them. We agreed to try the assignment again the following week.

This time she arrived early and announced in the waiting room, before we entered my office, "I haven't told a lie all week!" She rushed to look at herself. "Hmm," she said softly, then turned to me and asked, "Do you see anything?"

"I see a girl who has chosen to be honest for a week."

But she persisted, "Do I look different?" I suggested she turn back to the mirror and decide for herself. "I do look happier," she announced.

"Well, that's a difference, isn't it?"

Then I suggested that we find out what would happen if she came home each day precisely at the time she had told her parents she would.

Our next session revolved partly about her parents. "My parents had the most terrible fight."

This did not surprise me. "About you?" I asked.

"No, about their relationship." Then she sat down in front of the mirror and said to her reflection, "You see what happens when they don't have you to fight about?" I was pleased by her insight and remained silent. "I think I'm getting prettier," she declared. That was her way of telling me that she had successfully carried out her assignment to keep her word.

In a subsequent session we did some sentence-completion work. Here were her responses to the stem **I like myself most when I—**

> *am not trying to be like everybody else.*
> *do what I say I'll do.*
> *don't goof off in class.*
> *do my homework.*
> *tell the truth.*

have fun with my dad.
use my brains instead of pretending I'm stupid.
keep out of trouble.
walk away from smoking pot.

I like myself least when I—

play dumb.
act helpless.
throw a tantrum to get attention.
overeat.
act impulsively.
don't put out my opinions with people.
lie.
break promises.

During this period I conducted several parallel sessions with Eva's parents, alerting them to the fact that as she changed and improved, they might experience more difficulties in their marriage, since Eva would no longer provide a distraction. In fact, I warned them, they might very well sabotage her progress so as to avoid confronting the problems in their marriage. We agreed to meet at regular intervals, with Eva and her brother present, to monitor the family's response to Eva's changes. Thus, her desire for attention was now being fulfilled, but in ways that were beneficial to all members of her family. We had engaged her sense of worth (plus her sense of her lovableness, plus her view of her attractiveness) with her honesty and integrity.

As Eva learned to live more responsibly, her self-esteem rose. She liked herself more. Her desire to live responsibly became stronger. Her school grades improved. She became more discriminating about both her friends and her activities. She and her brother became better friends. One of the results of Eva's counseling was that her parents saw how their own problems contributed to Eva's difficulties. They sought marriage counseling.

Eva learned to differentiate between the traits she admired in her parents and those she did not. She became more discriminating about which traits she emulated, and she rejected those traits that she sensed her parents themselves felt guilty about. Her parents breathed a sigh of relief as this became apparent. They lost some of the guilt they were experiencing as parents and learned to support her efforts to grow into a strong, dependable adult.

In assisting Eva to strengthen her self-esteem, the most important step was the first: she needed to *give up lying*. Not only was she lying to others about her actions, she was lying to herself about who she was, pretending an inadequacy that belied her potential. A great deal of other work was needed, but her willingness to experiment with truthfulness was essential for the beginning of change.

Is there any aspect of Eva's psychology that might have relevance to you?

I trust the reader understands that in my telling of these stories I have omitted a great deal. This is not a book about the art of psychotherapy. The stories are simplified to keep in clear focus the main points relevant to our purposes. They are offered to help us understand that who and what we think we are influences how we act—to help us appreciate the awesome power of self-concept.

What we are chiefly concerned with is what we as adults can do to raise the level of our self-esteem, to learn to love and trust ourselves more, and to have greater assurance about our effectiveness.

True, some of us may need psychotherapy to resolve fully our difficulties. But most of us *can* do a good deal on our own, provided we are willing to make the effort. The situation is somewhat like the issue of physical exercise: it is undeniably easier with a coach or trainer, but, with proper guidance from a book, we *can* produce a major improvement in our condition. It comes down to a question of will and determination.

We want to succeed with our lives. We want for ourselves the best that is realistically possible. If self-esteem is the key, how do we generate it?

Chapter 3
Living Consciously

There are two words that best describe what we can do to raise our self-esteem—to generate more self-confidence and self-respect. They are: *Live consciously.* The problem with this statement is that it may be too abstract for some people; it does not self-evidently translate into mental and/or physical action. And if we wish to grow, we need to know *what to do.* We need to learn *new behaviors.* So we must ask: If we practiced living more consciously, in what ways would we be *acting differently*?

We will need the balance of this book to answer this question fully, but first let's see why living consciously is the foundation of self-confidence and self-respect.

Our minds are our basic means of survival. *All our distinctively human accomplishments are the reflections of our ability to think.* Successful life depends on the appropriate use of intelligence—appropriate, that is, to the tasks and goals we set for ourselves and to the challenges we face. This is the core biological fact of our existence.

But the appropriate use of our consciousness is not automatic: rather, *it is an act of choice.* We are free to strive for the expansion or the contraction of consciousness. We can seek to see more or to see less. We can wish to know or not to know. We can struggle for clarity or for fog. We can live consciously or semiconsciously or (for most practical purposes) *unconsciously.* This is the ultimate meaning of free will.

If our lives and well-being depend on the appropriate use of consciousness, then the extent to which we honor sight over blindness is the single most important determinant of our self-confidence and self-respect. We can hardly feel competent in life while wandering around (at work, or in our marriages, or in dealing with our children) in a self-induced mental fog. If we betray our basic means of survival by attempting to exist unthinkingly, our sense of worthiness suffers accordingly, regardless of other people's approval or disapproval of us. *We* know our defaults, whether or not anyone else does. *Self-esteem is the reputation we acquire with ourselves.*

A thousand times a day we must choose the level of consciousness at which we will function. A thousand times a day we must choose between thinking and nonthinking. Gradually, over time, we establish a sense of the kind of person we are, depending on the choices we make, the rationality and integrity we exhibit. That is the reputation of which I speak.

The more intelligent we are, the greater is our potential for awareness, but the principle of living consciously remains the same regardless of level of intelligence. To live consciously means to seek to be aware of everything that bears on our actions, purposes, values, and goals, and to behave in accordance with that which we see and know.

In any given situation, living consciously means generating a state of mind appropriate to the task at hand. Driving a car, making love, writing a grocery list, studying a balance sheet, meditating—all require somewhat different mind states, different kinds of mental processes. *In matters of mental functioning, context determines appropriateness.* Living consciously means taking responsibility for the awareness appropriate to the action in which we are engaged. This, above all, is the foundation of self-confidence and self-respect.

Self-esteem, then, is a function, not of what we are born with, but of *how we use our consciousness*—the choices we make concerning awareness, the honesty of our relationship to reality, and the level of our personal integrity. A person of high intelligence and high self-esteem does not feel *more* appropriate to life or *more* worthy of happiness than a person of high self-esteem and modest intelligence.

Living consciously implies respect for the facts of reality—the facts of our inner world as well as of the outer world—as contrasted with an attitude that amounts to: "If I don't choose to see it or acknowledge it, it doesn't exist." Living consciously is living *responsibly toward reality.*

This doesn't mean that we have to like what we see, but it does mean we recognize that which is and that which is not, and that wishes or fears or denials do not alter facts.

To illustrate what I mean by living consciously, I offer the following examples.

Living consciously. When John was hired for a new job, he did everything he could to master what was required of him and kept looking for ways to perform his tasks more efficiently. Beyond that, he sought to understand the wider context in which his work took place, so that he would be qualified to move up and not be stuck indefinitely on the level where he started. His basic desire was *to learn*—and thereby to keep growing in confidence, productiveness, and competence.

Living unconsciously. When Jim was hired for a job with the same firm, he imagined that if he memorized the routine of the tasks assigned to him and didn't attract negative attention, he might hope for security. *Challenges* had no appeal for him, since they entailed risk and required thought. He operated at the minimal level of awareness necessary to repeat the motions he had been taught, contributing nothing of his own. His gaze rarely strayed from his work station, except for purposes of socializing or daydreaming. He felt no curiosity about his job in the wider sense. Why should he? he felt; the job was there. He kept a small clock in front of him so that he would know precisely when it was five o'clock, time to go home. When he was confronted by his supervisor with mistakes he had made, he typically alibied and inwardly seethed. But when John was promoted and Jim was not, Jim felt bewildered and resentful.

Which of these two behavior patterns more resembles yours? And what is the impact of this behavior on your self-esteem?

Living consciously. A happily married woman named Serena once said to me, "An hour after I met the man I married, I could have given you a lecture on the ways he would be difficult to live with. I think he's the most exciting man I've ever known, but I've never kidded myself about the fact that he's also one of the most self-absorbed. Often he's like an absentminded professor. He spends a great deal of time in a private world of his own. I had to know that going in, or else I would have been very upset later. He never made any pretenses about the kind of man he was. I can't understand people who profess to be hurt or shocked at the way their mates turn out. It's so obvious what people are if you'll just *pay attention*. I've never been happier in my whole life than I am right now in this marriage, but not because I tell myself my husband is 'perfect' or 'without fault.' You know, I think that's why I feel so appreciative of his strength and virtues. *I'm willing to see everything."*

Living unconsciously. A woman named Carol who came for psychotherapy said at our first session, "I have the most awful bad luck with men. I mean, how many women can say that their last three lovers all beat them? I don't know why these things happen. Why me, God, why me? No, I can't say I take the trouble to get to know a man before . . . you know. I mean, part of the excitement is being in a daze, isn't it? It's always a big shock—I can't believe it's happening!—I mean, when they start swinging. Oh, I suppose I kind of knew . . . in a way . . . they were going to be trouble. There were signs. But I *wanted* things to be good! I *wanted* each one to be Mr. Right. So, even if I heard how they treated other women, I told myself, 'He'll be different with me.' I wonder if the other women told themselves that, too. . . . Mother used to say, 'Look before you leap.' But can you have fun that way? I like to just close my eyes . . . and fall. Come what may!—that's my philosophy. If only I'd meet a better type of man."

Granted, these two women represent the extremes of opposite attitudes. But in your personal relationships, which attitude is closer to your own?

Living consciously. When Roger was growing up, he saw and heard many things he could not understand. He heard his mother lecture him on the virtue of honesty and then, on many occasions, heard her lie to the neighbors.

He saw his father look at his mother with hatred a moment after saying to her, "Yes, dear, you're right, I apologize." He saw that most adults almost never told the truth about their feelings; that they usually looked unhappy and defeated, but that that did not prevent them from delivering sermons on how to live a successful life. They seemed to care much more about what other people thought than about what was right. He was dismayed and at times frightened by what he saw; but he kept on looking, kept on trying to understand. He knew he did not want to be like the grown-ups around him. He often felt lonely for someone he could truly admire. But he did not pretend that he admired the people he knew. He was impatient to grow up so that he could go out and find a better path than that offered by the adults he saw. In the meantime, he told himself, nothing was more important than to protect the clarity of his own sight . . . and not to surrender to hopelessness. Bruised, battered, alienated from those around him, he hung on, he persevered—and grew up to discover friends he *could* like and admire, and possibilities for the kind of life he had dreamed of as a child, when he didn't even know the words to name it. As an adult, he found the words—and the reality.

Living unconsciously. Milton lived in a world very much like Roger's, but very early in life he drew a different conclusion. Dimly and wordlessly he decided: Seeing too much is dangerous. He wanted to belong, he wanted to be loved, and that felt more important than anything else. So he pretended not to notice when grown-ups were lying or being hypocritical or cruel, and he learned to emulate their behavior. A day came when it felt as natural as breathing. By the time he was a teenager, he wondered what had happened to the excitement he had felt as a little boy; but he quickly pushed such thoughts from his mind. When he was twenty years old, his father said to him one day, "Do you think life is about being happy?" By now Milton was so numb he knew no answer was required; his father was merely stating the obvious. Having a drink with his friends, when he was thirty, Milton said, "I'll tell you the secret of life: Go through the motions and don't think. Then you don't feel the pain." Everyone felt that Milton was a regular fellow, except his bewildered children, who saw a void staring at them from his eyes. But to adults he appeared entirely normal, which is what Milton had always wanted, and would sell his soul for, and did.

Can you relate the psychology of either of these men to yourself? If you can, what is illuminated?

Living consciously. Karen was a research scientist in the field of biochemistry. She had written several highly regarded papers in which she developed a theory that was gaining a great many adherents among her colleagues. Then, in an obscure journal published in Australia, she read of some experimental findings that, if verified, completely invalidated her theory. She duplicated the experiments, found that her theory was indeed disconfirmed, and published a paper announcing this. When a more cynical associate asked her why she would choose to set back her own career on the basis of a lead from a journal no one had ever heard of, she looked at him uncomprehendingly, which only infuriated her colleague. "I'm interested in what is *true*," she said. "What is truth?" shrugged her colleague.

Living unconsciously. In this case, it would be to share the mentality of the colleague in the story above, regardless of one's profession.

Of these two conflicting attitudes toward truth, which

one more resembles your own? And how consistent are you? And how is your sense of yourself affected?

Living consciously. In the midst of a heated argument with his wife, Jerry stopped suddenly and said, "Wait a minute. I think I'm being defensive and not really hearing you. Could we back up a few steps and try again? Now let me see if I understand what you're saying."

Living unconsciously. For years Phillip's wife had tried to tell him she was unhappy in their marriage. His typical response was to become uncontrollably sleepy. When she attempted to have a discussion with him early in the day, in the hope that he would be more awake, he snapped, "Why do you always start these impossible subjects when you know I'm getting ready to go to work?" When his wife asked for an alternative time that would be more suitable, he responded, "Now you're trying to trap me! I can't stand pressure!" When his wife told him that unless they learned to communicate, she was unprepared to spend her life with him, he yelled, "Do you think other wives are any happier?" and stormed out of the house. When, after years of such nonconfrontations, he came home one day to find her gone, and a note saying that she couldn't take it anymore, he cried to an empty house, "What's the matter? How could this have happened? How could she just leave without giving me a chance?"

Do you identify with one of these patterns of behavior more than the other? Can you find aspects of yourself in these two stories? And do you like or dislike what you see?

Living consciously. Whenever Kay decided on a new goal, she immediately asked herself what would be required to attain it. When she wanted to start her own business, she prepared an elaborate plan of action, including a series of detailed substrategies that allowed her to move step by step toward her desired end; and then she proceeded to act. She did not wait passively for someone to provide her with the fulfillment of her dreams. When something went wrong, her typical response was, "What did I overlook?" When she encountered obstacles, she thought not in terms of blame but in terms of solutions. She took responsibility for being the *cause* of the *effects* she wanted. When she succeeded, she was not astonished.

Living unconsciously. Mary was unhappy working in a dress shop and dreamed of having a shop of her own. But when friends asked her why and how she thought she could make a go of it, she answered, "But wouldn't it be wonderful?" When her boss reproached her for daydreaming on the job and being careless and inattentive with customers, she told herself, "It's hard to concentrate on unimportant things when I'm thinking about my own ambitions." When a friend suggested that it would be helpful if she showed more initiative at her job, she answered, "Why should I kill myself working for somebody else?" On hearing from her employer that her services were no longer required, she felt shocked and betrayed. She wondered why some people seemed to realize their dreams while she could not, and she thought, "Maybe I'm just not unscrupulous enough to succeed in business." She was vaguely aware of the hatred growing in her heart, but she called it "indignation at the injustice of 'the system.' "

If you knew two such women, which would you have more in common with? Which more reminds you of yourself? And can you see the implications for your self-confidence and self-respect?

* * *

Living consciously. Elizabeth loved her husband, who was a builder; and when she learned that he was cutting corners on some of his construction projects in order to keep costs down, in ways that bordered on the unethical, she was distraught. She knew that times were bad in the building industry and that the competition was ferocious. But her preoccupation with her own work prevented her from realizing how worried her husband was about his business. When Elizabeth broached the subject with him, at first he was angry and defensive. But when she persevered, and he saw that she was concerned rather than hostile, he proceeded more and more to share with her his anxieties and the considerations that were prompting his "corner cutting." Even so, they went through many difficult hours in the next week; at times each lost control and resorted to shouting. But in the end, reason, love, and mutual respect won out; he committed himself to correcting his recent breaches on the job and to practicing the integrity he had exhibited in the past. His wife reinforced his confidence that he would find a way to prevail. Having successfully weathered another storm, their marriage became stronger. "If you really love someone," Elizabeth said, "you don't let fear stop you from challenging him when that's what the situation calls for."

Living unconsciously. Louise did not feel comfortable about her husband's new prospective partner when Paul brought him home for dinner. Paul owned several automobile service garages that were currently short of necessary capital, which this man was proposing to provide in exchange for a share of the business. None of the conversation at the dinner table made sense to Louise and she did not attempt to bring it into clear focus; she told herself that business is a man's work and she should not attempt to think about it. Nonetheless, it seemed to her, if only dimly, that the man was saying that while *on paper* he would now be the majority owner, *in fact* the business would remain Paul's. "After all," the man said, "what do I know about service garages?" She noticed that Paul seemed restless, distracted, and vaguely irritable whenever she spoke. She told herself that a wife's foremost duty is to keep the home peaceful, so she remained dutifully silent. She tuned out the rest of the conversation. She said nothing when she saw Paul sign the agreement papers without checking with his lawyer, and she chose not to think about it, either; just as she chose not to think when she saw one employee after another being discharged, on the orders of the new partner, and less-experienced ones being hired without Paul's being consulted; just as she chose not to think or to speak about it when she saw Paul's income shrinking for no reasons he could explain to her; just as she chose not to think or to speak about it when Paul came home one day and announced that he was filing for personal bankruptcy. It was as if each blow were a signal to close down her consciousness still further. By now she was crying a good deal—in fact, they both were— but they were not speaking or thinking about it. "What's there to think about?" Paul said one day in answer to her silence. "I had some bad luck. It could happen to anybody." Louise looked at him across the breakfast table, desperately keeping her mind wrapped in fog so that she would not start screaming. But she felt betrayed, not so much by her husband as by her parents, who long ago had promised her that if a woman is compliant and supportive and never challenges her husband, she will be happy. But Louise was not happy. *Why had life cheated her?* she wondered bitterly. "Perhaps Paul will do something," she told herself. It was not in her or Paul's view of existence that husbands and wives might think and talk together about the issues of their life.

Can you find aspects of yourself in either of these women? If so, identify what they are. Are you proud or sad about what you identify?

Living consciously. When Norman reached the age of forty-two, he knew he had achieved the major goals he had set for himself. He was happily married, he was a physician with a successful practice, and he had three children he loved and was proud of. But he was becoming increasingly aware of a vague dissatisfaction rising from deep within, as if some unknown part of his self was trying to get a signal through to his conscious mind. At first, all he could identify was a diffuse sense of longing. He did not brush it aside; he watched it. Gradually he found himself remembering a long-forgotten dream of his youth: to write books. He reduced his work schedule and his social life to permit more time to explore these dreams and yearnings. He could not tell, at first, whether they represented a real desire or the residue of an adolescent fantasy; but he knew it was important to find out, because he knew that his life and what he made of it were important. He began to see that he passionately wanted to write fiction. Soon he was working on the outline of a novel. Two years later the novel was finished; a year and a half after that, it was published. It did only moderately well. But by now Norman knew beyond doubt that this was the work he wanted. His second novel was more successful, his third more successful still. He retired from medicine to write full-time. Watching him, his wife saw Norman grow younger and happier. Watching him, his children learned an invaluable lesson: honor your own wants; honor your own life. "Always be alert to your inner signals," he said to them. "Don't act impulsively, but *pay attention*. Sometimes one part of our mind is years ahead of another part in its wisdom."

Living unconsciously. Tim was bored. A psychologist who had opened his practice at the age of twenty-eight, he was now fifty-one, and he wondered how he could stand another twenty or so years of the same work. He had an individual and a group practice and occasionally he conducted seminars for industry. He could no longer remember the point at which he had ceased working for pleasure and begun working solely for money, but he knew that pleasure had ceased to be relevant long ago. Once he had offered his clients excitement; now he offered tired, cynical "wisdom." He felt like a fraud and was continually astonished that no one else seemed to notice. It occurred to him, vaguely, that clients came to him with just such problems as he was now experiencing. But that did not motivate him to think about his situation or to discuss it with anyone. His favorite recreation and escape was tennis, and often when a client was talking to him and he felt bored he dreamed of tennis. To his family he seemed more and more lifeless, withdrawn, and irritable. Finally, he became enamored of a female client thirty years his junior and disappeared with her to an ashram in Colorado led by an Indian guru who taught "free love" and drug "experimentation"—together with absolute submission to the will of the guru—as a path of spiritual enlightenment. The guru told him that thinking had been the cause of all of Tim's troubles, and Tim liked to believe that this was true.

Two different attitudes toward life, reason, and reality. Which is closer to your own? And what do you observe to be the consequences for your self-esteem?

* * *

In considering the preceding examples, observe the kind of issues involved in living consciously versus living unconsciously:

Thinking, even when thinking is difficult, versus nonthinking

Awareness, even when awareness is challenging, versus unawareness

Clarity, whether or not it comes easily, versus obscurity or vagueness

Respect for reality, whether pleasant or painful, versus avoidance of reality

Respect for truth versus rejection of truth

Independence versus dependence

Active orientation versus passive orientation

Willingness to take appropriate risks, even in the face of fear, versus unwillingness

Honesty with self versus dishonesty

Living in and being responsible to the present versus retreating into fantasy

Self-confrontation versus self-avoidance

Willingness to see and correct mistakes versus perseverance in error

Reason versus irrationalism

In the preceding stories, you will find all these themes present implicitly.

One of the most important issues entailed in living consciously is intellectual independence. A person cannot think through the mind of another. We can learn from one another, but real knowledge implies understanding, not mere repetition or imitation. We can either exercise our own minds or pass on to others the responsibility of knowledge and evaluation and accept their verdicts more or less uncritically.

Of course, we are sometimes influenced by others in ways we do not recognize. But this does not alter the fact that there is a distinction between the psychology of those who try to understand things for themselves, and those who do not. What is crucial here is our intention, our goal. As a matter of general policy, do you *aim* to think for yourself? Is that your basic orientation?

To speak of "thinking independently" is useful because the redundancy has value in terms of emphasis. Often what people call "thinking" is merely recycling the opinions of others, not true thinking at all. Thinking independently—about our work, our relationships, the values that will guide our lives—is part of what is meant by living consciously.

Independence is a self-esteem virtue.

In considering the preceding vignettes, you may wish to ask: Don't these people who live consciously already have good self-esteem, and don't the people who live unconsciously lack good self-esteem? How, then, can living consciously be *the foundation* of good self-esteem?

We encounter here what I call *the principle of reciprocal causation*. By this I mean that behaviors that generate good self-esteem are also expressions of good self-esteem. Behaviors that are expressions of good self-esteem are also generators of good self-esteem. Living consciously is both a cause and an effect of self-confidence and self-respect.

The more I live consciously, the more I trust my mind

and respect my worth. The more I trust my mind and respect my worth, the more natural it feels to live consciously. This same relationship exists among all behaviors that support self-esteem.

Think about these stories. Can you isolate the areas in your life where you operate with the most consciousness? How about the areas where you operate with the least consciousness? Using the material in this chapter for guidance, prepare two such lists in a notebook. This is an excellent way to deepen your understanding of what the issue of living consciously means for you.

Now, let us say you identify three areas in which you recognize that your average level of consciousness is far less than it should be. Meditate on what seems to be difficult about staying in high-level mental focus in these areas. Then, for each of these areas, write **The hard thing about staying fully conscious here is**— and then, as rapidly as possible, without censoring yourself or "thinking," write six to ten endings. Then do the same for **The good thing about not being fully conscious here is**—. Then follow with **If I were to stay fully conscious here**—. You will probably make some illuminating discoveries. In doing the exercise, you will already be living more consciously.

Finally, give some thought to tomorrow—and the next seven days of your life. Consider the question of how you can apply these ideas to your daily concerns. If, for example, you choose to be more conscious at work, what might you do differently? If you choose to be more conscious in one or more of your relationships, what would change in your behavior? If you wish to grow in self-confidence and self-respect, *begin now*. Identify three new behaviors in the realms of work and relationships, respectively, that you can practice this week—and commit yourself to experimenting with them.

And then go on working in the next seven days, and the next, to expand your consciousness further, one small step at a time. In the arena of raising self-esteem, we evolve, not by dreaming of giant steps, but by committing ourselves *in action* to little ones, moving step by relentless step to an ever-expanding field of vision.

Not that extraordinary breakthroughs and transformations cannot occur. They can—but not to those who wait in empty passivity. We must act, and we must begin from where we are. One small shift to higher consciousness opens the door to another—and another. It does not matter at what point we start; it matters only that we take the responsibility of starting.

Chapter 4
Learning Self-Acceptance

If the essence of living consciously is respect for facts and reality, then self-acceptance is its ultimate test. When the facts we must face have to do with ourselves, living consciously can suddenly become very difficult. Here is where the challenge of self-acceptance enters.

Self-acceptance asks that we approach our experience with an attitude that makes the concepts of approval or disapproval irrelevant: the desire to see, to know, *to be aware.*

Now, to be self-accepting does not mean to be without a desire to change, improve, or evolve. The truth is that self-acceptance is a precondition of change. If we accept the fact of what we feel and what we are, at any given moment of our existence, we can permit ourselves to be aware fully of the nature of our choices and actions, and our development is not blocked.

Let us begin with a simple example. Stand in front of a full-length mirror and look at your face and body. Notice your feelings as you do so. Probably you will like some parts of what you see more than others. If you are like most people, you will find some parts difficult to look at for long, because they agitate or displease you. Perhaps you see a pain in your face you do not want to confront. Perhaps there is some aspect of your body you so dislike that you can hardly bear to keep your eyes focused there. Perhaps you see signs of age and cannot bear to stay connected with the thoughts and emotions those signs evoke. So the impulse is to escape—to flee from consciousness—to reject, deny, disown aspects of your self.

But stay focused on your image in the mirror a few moments longer, and experiment with saying to yourself, "Whatever my defects or imperfections, I accept myself unreservedly and completely." Stay focused, breathe deeply, and say this over and over again for a minute or two, without rushing the process. Rather, allow yourself to experience fully the meaning of your words. You may find yourself protesting, "But I don't *like* certain things about my body—so how can I accept unreservedly and completely?" But remember: "accepting" does not necessarily mean "liking"; "accepting" does not mean we cannot imagine or wish for changes or improvements. It means experiencing, without denial or avoidance, that a fact is a fact; in this case, it means accepting that the face and body in the mirror are *your* face and body, and that they are what they are. If you persist, if you surrender to reality, if you surrender to awareness (which is what "accepting" ultimately means) you may notice that you have begun to relax a bit, and perhaps feel more comfortable with yourself, and more real.

Even though you may not like or enjoy everything that you see when you look in the mirror, you are still able to say, "Right now, that's me. And I don't deny the fact. I accept it." That is respect for reality.

Do this exercise for two minutes every morning and every night, and within a very short time you will begin to experience the relationship between self-acceptance and self-esteem: a mind that honors sight honors itself.

And you will make another important discovery: Not only will you be in a more harmonious relationship to yourself, not only will you grow in self-confidence and self-respect, but if there are aspects of your self that you do not like and that are within your power to change, you will be more motivated to make the changes once you have accepted the facts as they now are. *We are not moved to change those things whose reality we deny.*

Our self-esteem is not a function of our physical attractiveness, as some people naively imagine. But our willingness or unwillingness to see and accept ourselves does have consequences for self-esteem. Our attitude toward the person we see in the mirror is only one example of the issue of self-acceptance. Let us consider others.

Suppose you are about to give a talk to a group of people and you are afraid. Or you are about to enter a party where you know only a few people and you are feeling insecure or shy. You are distressed by your anxiety and you try to fight it the way most people do: by tensing your body, contracting your breathing, and telling yourself, "Don't be afraid (or shy)." This strategy does not work. In fact, it makes your discomfort worse. Your body is now sending your brain the signals of an emergency alert, the signals of danger—to which you typically respond by "fighting" your disquietude still more ferociously, with tension, with oxygen deprivation, and perhaps with anger and self-reproach. You are at war with yourself—because you do not know what else to do. No one has ever taught you, and you have never learned, that an alternative strategy exists that is far more helpful. It is the strategy of self-acceptance.

In this strategy, you do not fight the feeling of distress; rather, you breathe into it, accept it. Perhaps you tell yourself, "Boy, am I afraid," and then you take a long, slow, deep breath. You concentrate on breathing gently and deeply, even though this is difficult at first and may remain difficult for some time; you persevere; and you watch your fear, become a witness to it, without identifying with it, without allowing it to define you. "If I'm afraid, I'm afraid—but that's no reason to go unconscious. Let me continue to use my eyes. Let me continue to *see.*" You may even choose to "talk" to your fear, inviting it to tell you the worst imaginable that could happen, so that that can be faced and accepted too—a strategy that tends to bring you out of self-tormenting fantasies and into far more benign reality. You may become aware of when and how this fear began in you. You may appreciate more deeply that it is groundless, that it is, in effect, an obsolete response having no real relevance to the present. By accepting it completely, you may find that you are released from the past *into the present.* Your fear may not always disappear—sometimes it will, sometimes it will only diminish—but you will be *relatively* more relaxed and freer to act effectively.

We are always stronger when we do not try to fight reality. We cannot make our fear go away by yelling at it, or yelling at ourselves, or indulging in self-rebuke. But if we can open to our experience, stay conscious, and remember that we are larger than any one emotion, we can at minimum begin to transcend unwanted feelings, and often we can dispel them, since full, sincere acceptance tends, in time, to dissolve negative or unwanted feelings such as pain, anger, envy, or fear.

If a person is afraid, it is usually futile to tell him or her to "relax." The person does not know how to translate that advice into behavior. But if you speak of gently deepening the breathing, or of imagining what it might feel like not to fight the fear, then you are proposing an "actable"—that is, something a person can *do*. A person should think of expanding to allow the fear in, even of welcoming the fear, making friends with it—or at least watch it without identifying with it—and finally project the worst that might happen and then face that. One can certainly learn to say, "I am feeling fear, and I can accept that fact, but I am *more* than my fear." In other words, do not *identify* with the fear. Think, "I recognize my fear and I accept it . . . and now let me see if I can remember how my body feels when I am *not* afraid." This is a very powerful device for handling fear (or any other unwanted feeling). These are actions you can learn, rehearse in imagination, and practice when fear situations arise.

The practice I am describing is appropriate for virtually any fear. It is useful in the dentist's chair, or when preparing to ask for a raise, or when facing a difficult interview, or when having to tell someone painful information, or when grappling with fears of rejection or abandonment.

When you learn to accept fear, you cease making a catastrophe of it. Then it ceases to be your master. You are no longer tortured by fantasies that may bear little or no relation to reality. You are free to see people and situations as they are. You feel more efficacious. You feel more in control of your life. Self-confidence and self-respect rise.

Self-esteem rises through this process, even when fears are not the product of irrational fantasies but in fact the particular reality you have to confront *is* dreadful. I had a good friend who, some years ago, was hit by devastating cancer. At the time, I thought her bravery in coping with it was extraordinary. I remember a day, visiting her in the hospital, when she told me this story: Her doctors had told her radiation therapy was necessary. The prospect terrified her. She asked if she could go to the radiation room for a few minutes each day, for three days, before treatment began. "I just want to look at the machine," she told her doctors. "Make friends with it. Then I'll be ready. I won't be afraid." She said to me, "I just sat looking at the machine . . . accepting it . . . accepting my situation . . . and meditating on the fact that the machine existed to *help* me. It made the treatment so much easier." Eventually, she died. But I will never forget her serenity and her dignity. She knew how to value herself. It is as beautiful an illustration of the principle of acceptance as I have ever seen.

Take a few minutes to contemplate some feeling or emotion of yours that is not easy for you to face—insecurity, pain, envy, rage, sorrow, humiliation, fear. When you isolate the feeling, see if you can bring it into clearer focus, perhaps by thinking of or imagining whatever typically evokes it. Then breathe into the feeling, as if opening your body to it. Imagine what it would feel like not to resist this feeling but to accept it fully. Explore that experience. Take your time.

Practice saying to yourself, "I am now feeling such and such (whatever the feeling is) and I accept it fully." At first, this may be difficult; you may find that you tense your body in protest. But persevere; concentrate on your breathing; think of giving your muscles permission to let go of their tension; remind yourself, "A fact is a fact; that which is, is; if the feeling exists, it exists." Keep contemplating the feeling. Think of *allowing* the feeling to be there (rather than trying to wish or will it out of existence). You may find it useful, as I have, to tell yourself, "I am now exploring the world of fear or pain or envy or confusion (or whatever)."

In so doing, you will be exploring the world of self-acceptance.

I was once in a physician's office where I had to take a series of rather painful injections. In response to the shock and pain of the first needle, I stopped breathing and contracted my whole body, as if to hold off an invading army. But of course tensing my muscles made penetration more difficult and therefore made the experience more painful. My wife, Devers, who was in the office receiving the same injections, noticed this and said to me, "As you feel the needle touch your skin, breathe in, as if drawing the needle in with your breath. Imagine that you are welcoming the needle." I immediately realized that this is precisely what I teach people to do with emotions, so I did what Devers proposed—and the needle entered with almost negligible discomfort. I *accepted* the needle—*and any attendant feelings*—rather than treat them as adversaries.

This strategy is very familiar, of course, to athletes and dancers, whose work requires them to "ride with" pain rather than convulse against it. And the Lamaze breathing exercises taught to pregnant women for controlling and easing pain, anxiety, and body reactions embody precisely the principle we are considering here.

In therapy I sometimes work with women who have difficulty experiencing orgasm during intercourse. Since fear often acts to inhibit pleasure, and therefore orgasm, and since fear often triggers the response of cutting off breathing and contracting the muscles—as if defending against the "invading" penis—I teach women to reverse this process. Women learn to *breathe in* as the penis enters, *to accept the penis*. They learn to expand in welcome rather than contract in rejection. In doing so, they learn to accept and achieve a higher degree of comfort and pleasure in intercourse because they are surrendering to the experience rather than fighting it. The result is a far greater sexual enjoyment. In the process, of course, fantasies of being hurt or destroyed by the penis, or of falling dangerously out of control, tend to disappear. A woman able to allow herself orgasms clearly is more in control than one who is incapacitated by fear. The point is, acceptance releases us into reality.

The principle we need to remember remains the same, whether it is fear or pleasure we are contracting against: *Do not be in an adversarial relationship to your own experience.* If you permit an adversarial relationship to develop, you intensify negatives while depriving yourself of positives.

Following are four illustrations of situations where people choose to practice either self-acceptance or self-disowning.

Practicing self-acceptance. Lucian began to notice that he was sexually attracted to his next-door neighbor. He considered himself a happily married man, and his initial reaction was to reproach himself. But soon he decided that it was better to understand himself than to practice blind self-rebuke. He allowed himself to experience (in his inner life) the sexual attraction. He paid attention to the feelings his neighbor evoked in him, and he permitted his fantasies free rein. Soon he became aware that it was not so much his neighbor he hungered for as new stimulation— and not because he was bored with his wife but because he was bored with his job. He saw that a new woman offered the promise of a moment's experience of *effectiveness*, which his work was no longer providing. He did not feel guilty; he regarded his response to his neighbor merely as a source of valuable information about frustrations within himself. He knew he would not betray his wife, but he did allow himself to imagine what an affair with his neighbor might be like. At dinner that evening, he said to his wife, "This afternoon, sitting by myself in the yard for an hour, I had an eight-month affair with the lady next door." The serenity and amusement of his manner told his wife that she had nothing to fear, so she inquired, "And how was it?" Lucian took his wife's hand and answered, "Frustrating. Pointless. It wasn't the answer. But I think finding a different kind of work might be."

Practicing self-disowning. What Lucian did not know was that his neighbor, Marcia, had erotic feelings for him, and since she regarded such feelings as sinful, she repressed them. She became more and more tense with her husband and children. She had fits of weeping she could not explain. When she occasionally crossed paths with Lucian, she was alternately rude and flirtatious, the way a child is flirtatious who does not yet fully know what she is doing. Marcia had been unhappy in her marriage for a long time, but she did not allow herself to confront that, since to her divorce meant humiliation and failure. Had she allowed herself to accept and examine her feelings for Lucian, and perhaps discussed them with her husband, she might have gained valuable insight into her condition. But as a girl she had been taught that to lust after another person in your heart is as wicked as committing adultery—and she did not want to be wicked, so the only solution she knew was unconsciousness. In the end, after years of misery and noncommunication, her husband divorced her. Feeling betrayed, abandoned, and victimized, Marcia pondered, "Why do the good people in this world always have to suffer?"

Can you relate anything in these two stories to yourself?

Practicing self-acceptance. Gina was devastated when, following her divorce, her children informed her that they preferred to live with their father. She knew she had been an impatient, unempathic, careless mother, and that her former husband had been a better nurturer to the children than she had been. This was not easy to admit, as it was very painful. But with the children gone she had many opportunities to be alone and to think about the past. "The truth is," she finally admitted to herself, "I never wanted to be a mother. I became one because I thought I was supposed to." She spent many silent hours meditating on her past choices, not for the purpose of self-criticism but for the purpose of self-understanding. She became able to accept that it was better for her children to be with their father. Then, slowly, she became able to face and accept something far more difficult, because it did violence to so much she had been taught: she was *happy* that her children had chosen to live with her former husband. She felt free and unencumbered for the first time in her life. Consequently, when she was with her children, and she chose to see them often, they encountered a happier and more affectionate mother than they had ever known before. When friends and relatives tried to make her feel guilty for being "an unnatural mother," she looked at them tranquilly and did not attempt to defend herself. She knew who she was and she accepted it, and that was all that mattered. "I regret my past mistakes," she told herself, "but I don't think the way to redeem myself is to make more of them by repudiating my wants and needs once again."

Practicing self-disowning. One day, when Jack was sixty-two, his twenty-five-year-old son, Mark, tried to talk to him about what it had been like to be Jack's son. "I was so frightened of you when I was little," said Mark. "You were so violent—I never knew when you were going to swing out and hit me." Jack snapped irritably, "I don't want to hear about this." Mark answered patiently, "Look, Dad, I know it's uncomfortable for you. You must think my intention is to reproach you and make you feel bad. It isn't. I want us to be friends. I want to understand where you were coming from, then. You must have been terribly unhappy." But Jack refused to listen; he neither denied nor admitted his past behaviors toward his son, as if he preferred that the facts be left in a kind of limbo, neither real nor unreal, but enveloped in impenetrable fog. Mark tried and tried again, but to no avail. "Why won't you listen?" he shouted to his father. "Why won't you accept the truth of the way things were?" One day his father yelled back, "Why won't *you* accept the fact that I'm never going to be the father you want?" The two men stared at each other in shocked silence, as if for one moment they glimpsed something about themselves that they would immediately proceed to forget. "It's not possible that I was as cruel as he says," Jack thought, slamming his mind shut against the possibility. "It's not possible that I'm out for blood," Mark thought, slamming his mind shut against the possibility. Soon, the shouting continued.

In considering the psychology of these two people, can you find aspects of yourself? If so, what are the consequences to your self-esteem?

* * *

Now let us consider this question: Suppose our negative reaction to some experience is so overwhelming that we feel we *cannot* practice self-acceptance? The feeling, thought, or memory is so distressing and agitating that acceptance feels out of the question. We feel powerless not to block and contract. The solution is not to try to resist our resistance. If we cannot accept a feeling (or a thought or a memory), we should *accept our resistance*. In other words, start by accepting where we are. If we stay with the resistance at a conscious level, *it will begin to dissolve*.

If we can accept the fact that right now, at this moment, we *refuse* to accept that we feel envy, or anger, or pain, or longing, for example—or that we *refuse* to accept that we once did or believed such and such—if we acknowledge, experience, and accept our resistance—we discover a supremely important paradox: the resistance begins to collapse. When we fight a block it grows stronger; when we acknowledge and accept it, it begins to melt *because its continued existence requires opposition*.

Sometimes in therapy when a person has difficulty accepting some feeling, I will ask if he or she is willing to accept the fact of *refusing* to accept the feeling. I asked this once of a client, Victor, a clergyman who had great difficulty in owning or experiencing his anger, but who was a very angry man. My question disoriented him. "Will I accept that I won't accept my anger?" he asked me. I smiled and said, "That's right." He thundered, "I *refuse* to accept my anger and I *refuse* to accept my refusal!" I laughed and asked, "Will you accept your refusal to accept your refusal? We've got to begin somewhere. Let's begin there."

I asked him to face the group and say, "I'm not

angry," over and over again. Soon he was saying it very angrily indeed.

Then I had him say, "I *refuse* to accept my anger," which he shouted with escalating vigor.

Then I had him say, "I *refuse* to accept my refusal to accept my anger"—which he plunged into ferociously.

Then I had him say, "But I am willing to accept my refusal to accept my refusal," and he kept repeating it until, eventually, he broke down and joined in the laughter of the group.

"I get it." He grinned. "If you can't accept the experience, accept the resistance."

"Right. And if you can't accept the resistance, accept your resistance to accepting the resistance. The point is, eventually you'll arrive at a point you can accept. Then you can move forward from there."

Victor brightened. "When you experience resistance or denial with full consciousness, and embrace it, so to speak, you generate a kind of short circuit. A door swings open—and you're reconnected with your experience."

"That's it. So—are you angry?"

"I'm filled with anger."

"Can you accept that fact?"

"I don't like it."

"We all know that. But can you accept it?"

"I can accept it."

"Please look at me and say, 'Nathaniel, I'm really angry.'"

"Nathaniel, I'm really angry."

"Again, please."

"Nathaniel, I'm really angry."

"Good. Now we can begin to find out what you're angry about."

* * *

A powerful tool for cultivating self-awareness, self-acceptance, and personal growth is the sentence-completion procedure, which I wrote about in two earlier books, *If You Could Hear What I Cannot Say* and *To See What I See and Know What I Know*. One version of the procedure can serve us here. All that is required is a pen and a notebook.

At the top of a fresh page write one of the incomplete sentences, or sentence stems, I provide below. Follow the order of the stems as given. After you have written a stem at the top of a page, write six to ten endings as rapidly as you can. Do not worry if your ending is literally true, or if one ending conflicts with another. None of your endings is written in stone. It is merely an exercise—an experiment.

You may wish to tell yourself you can't do this. I assure you that you can. I have taught this procedure to many thousands of people and some of them always start out saying, "I can't"—and then proceed to do it.

At the top of the first page, write the stem: **Sometimes, looking back over my life, I can hardly believe that at one time I—**. Now write six to ten completions for that sentence. Go!

Then, on the next page, write: **It's not easy for me to admit that—** and then do your endings.

Then, on the next page, write: **It's not easy for me to be self-accepting when I—** and do the endings.

Then:

One of my emotions I have trouble accepting is—
One of my actions I have trouble accepting is—
One of the thoughts I tend to push out of my mind is—
One of the things about my body I have trouble accepting is—
If I were more accepting of my body—

If I were more accepting of things I have done—
If I were more accepting of my feelings—
If I were more honest about my wants and needs—
The scary thing about being self-accepting is—
If other people saw me being more self-accepting—
The good thing about being self-accepting might be—
I am becoming aware—
I am beginning to feel—
As I learn to stop denying my experience—
As I breathe deeply and allow myself to experience self-acceptance—

I must caution you: If you merely read these words and do not actually do the exercise as described, you will deprive yourself of discoveries I cannot otherwise make available to you.

I trust by now it has become clear why self-acceptance is essential to positive change. If I refuse to accept the fact that often I live unconsciously, how will I learn to live more consciously? If I refuse to accept the fact that often I live irresponsibly, how will I learn to live more responsibly? If I refuse to accept the fact that often I live passively, how will I learn to live more actively?

I cannot overcome a fear whose reality I deny. I cannot correct a sexual problem I will not admit exists. I cannot heal a pain I refuse to recognize as mine. I cannot change traits I insist I do not have. I cannot forgive myself for an action I will not acknowledge having taken.

To accept ourselves is to accept the fact that what we think, feel, and do are all expressions of the self *at the time they occur.*

But this does not mean that they are the final word on

who we are—unless we encase them in cement through our denials and disownings.

Allow me to share another personal example to further illuminate this issue.

Some years ago my wife Patrecia, whom I very much loved, died. For a long time my mind would endlessly review different aspects of our relationship. I would recall incidents when I had been thoughtless or unkind, and sometimes would push such memories away because they were unbearably painful. I did not deny the memories outright, but neither did I fully accept them and allow them and their implications to be assimilated and integrated. A part of myself was left fragmented, alienated from the rest of me.

Later I remarried, and while I am deeply and happily in love with my present wife, Devers, I saw certain patterns of thoughtlessness and lack of consideration repeating themselves. I began to reflect on a fact that I taught to other people: that if I could not fully accept the fact of some of my past behavior, it was almost inevitable that in one form or another I would repeat it. So I began to spend more time making real to myself certain actions I had taken, in my earlier marriage, such as failing to respond on some occasion when Patrecia needed my understanding or my help, or being overly impatient, or being excessively absorbed in work, the perfectly ordinary unkindnesses that love does not automatically prevent us from perpetrating. Making myself relive specific instances, reviewing detail by detail, was painful. Making myself look clearly at my actions was at times agitating beyond words, since Patrecia was gone and there was no way to make it up. But I knew that if I persisted—and of course if I achieved the same clarity regarding my behavior in my present marriage with Devers—two things would happen:

I would feel more integrated, and I would be less likely to repeat actions I would regret.

I invite you to consider some action of yours that you regret. See if you can drop self-blame while retaining the experience of yourself as the author of the action. Discover what it is like to accept that at some time in your life you chose to take that action. What does this form of honesty feel like? What are you learning about self-esteem?

After we accept the fact that our actions are *our* actions, there is still the issue of *assessment*—and we will have more to say in the next chapter about the process of assessing regretted behavior (thinking about it and interpreting its meaning) in a way that nurtures rather than undermines self-esteem. But this much I will say now: The errors we are willing to confront become the rungs of a ladder leading to higher self-esteem.

Anything that we have the possibility of experiencing, we have the possibility of disowning, either immediately or later, in memory. Anything that does not fit our official self-concept, or our official belief system, or that evokes anxiety for any reason whatever, we can reject.

I can refuse to accept my sensuality; I can refuse to accept my spirituality. I can disown my sorrow; I can disown my joy. I can repress the memory of actions I am ashamed of; I can repress the memory of actions I am proud of. I can deny my ignorance; I can deny my intelligence. I can refuse to accept my limitations; I can refuse to accept my potentials. I can conceal my weaknesses; I can conceal my strengths. I can deny my feelings of self-hatred; I can deny my feelings of self-love. I can pretend that I am more than I am; I can pretend that I am less than I am. I can disown my body; I can disown my mind.

The problem of non-self-acceptance is by no means confined to "negatives." We can be as frightened of our assets as of our shortcomings—as frightened of our genius, ambition, excitement, or beauty as of our emptiness, passivity, depression, or unattractiveness. Our liabilities pose the problem of inadequacy; our assets, the challenge of responsibility.

Our strengths or virtues can make us feel alone, alienated, cut off from the common herd, a target for envy and hostility, and our desire to *belong* can overcome any desire to actualize our highest potential. That many women, for example, associate high intelligence or achievement with loss of love or femininity is well known. It may take great courage to be willing to admit, even in the privacy of our own minds, "I can do things others don't seem able to do." Or, "I am more intelligent than anyone else in my family." Or, "I am unusually good-looking." Or, "I want more out of life than the people around me." Or, "I see farther and more clearly."

I recall a young woman who came to me for treatment many years ago. Lorraine was twenty-four years old, had the face of an angel, and swore like a longshoreman. She had experimented with every drug I had ever heard of and several I hadn't. When she was eighteen she had slept in the basement of a college fraternity house where she obtained food and shelter in exchange for sexual services. Now she was supporting herself as a waitress. Something made her pick up my book *The Psychology of Self-Esteem*, and it spoke to her: she called my office for an appointment.

She did everything she could to make me dislike her, but I liked her. I was convinced that she was hiding an extraordinary person behind a cloak of degradation. I remember one day when, with hypnosis, I age-regressed her to a day in junior high school. She began to weep. The teacher was asking questions at random of various pupils. I heard her whisper, "Please, God, if she asks me a question, please don't let me know the answer." I asked, "Why?" She answered, "Because they hate you. They hate you if you know too much. They hate you if you're too smart."

But she was not only unusually intelligent. As a young girl she had been tall for her age, physically strong, and unusually well coordinated. She could play almost any sport better than most boys, much to the anger and humiliation of her older brothers, who hit, ridiculed, and tormented her. Without looking at a book, she was an A student. In the small town in which she lived, there was no one like her, no one to talk to. She felt hated by her family, and *hated for her virtues*, not for her shortcomings.

As a teenager, she set out on a systematic course of self-destruction—as revenge against her family and, simultaneously, as a cry for help.

One day in therapy, when we had been working together for about six months, she became very angry with me. When she could not articulate her reasons, I invited her to do sentence completion.

The bad thing about you, Nathaniel, is—
you believe in me!
you refuse to see me as rotten!
you make me feel my pain!
you make me feel there's hope!
By now she was half-crying, half-snarling. She went on:
you make me believe in myself!

63

you brought me back to life!
you won't see me the way other people see me!
I hate you!

Now she was sobbing uncontrollably. "It's so hard," she cried, over and over again.

"What is?"

She looked at me with the fearful/hopeful eyes of a wild animal. "Admitting that what you see is there. That you're right. That I'm intelligent. That I'm special. That *I'm good.*"

Even now, almost two decades later, that moment remains with me as one of the great rewards of being a psychotherapist: the moment of seeing a human being summon the courage to admit and accept her own glory.

Eighteen months after entering therapy, she was studying creative writing at UCLA. A few years later, she was earning her living as a journalist and was married.

When I met her on the street by chance one day, about a decade after she had left therapy, I might not have recognized her if she had not come over and greeted me with a laughing hello. She was well dressed, self-assured, irresistibly cheerful, seemingly untouched by tragedy. "I don't know if you remember me, but I remember you."

I hesitated for a moment. "Is it . . . Lorraine?"

"Sure. That's me."

"How great to see you!"

"Do you know who you are, Nathaniel?"

"Who am I?"

"You're the man who refused to see me as a mongrel and a slut. You saw me as someone special. And you made me see it. God, there were times when I hated you so much! Accepting who I was, who I *really* was—that was the hardest thing I ever had to do in my whole life. People always talk about how hard it is to accept your faults. Somebody ought to talk about how hard it can be to accept your virtues."

Sometimes the path to higher self-esteem is lonely and frightening. We cannot fully know in advance how much more satisfying our lives will be. But the more we are willing to experience and accept the many different aspects of who we are, the richer our inner worlds, the greater our resources, the more appropriate we will feel to the challenges and opportunities of life. Also, it is more likely that we will find—or create—a style of existence that will meet our individual needs.

Thus far, we have dealt with self-acceptance as an application of rationality and realism; respect for our own experience; the refusal to be at war with ourselves. But there is another, deeper meaning to self-acceptance we need to consider.

I am referring to the courage required to admit that there is a place within us where—faults or no faults—*we like ourselves*. Many people find this a difficult idea to grasp.

Self-acceptance, in the ultimate sense, refers to an attitude of self-value and self-commitment that derives fundamentally from the fact that I am alive and conscious, that *I exist*. It is an experience deeper than self-esteem. It is a prerational, premoral act of self-affirmation, a kind of primitive egoism that is the birthright of every conscious organism, and yet that human beings have the power to act against or nullify.

Perhaps the following will help to make this issue clear.

Sometimes, after a client in therapy has expounded at length on his or her lack of self-esteem, and I want to evoke that other perspective, to which he or she seems to be oblivious, I will switch to sentence completion and ask the client to work with this stem: **If I were willing to admit how much I secretly like myself—**

And then, after a few protests from the client, I typically hear endings such as the following:

> *suppose other people don't agree?*
> *I would be embarrassed.*
> *I'd have to feel a lot of denied pain.*
> *you would be surprised.*
> *a lot of people would be shocked.*
> *I would be scared.*
> *my family wouldn't like it.*
> *I'd have no excuse for passivity.*
> *I could get on with my life.*

Then I might suggest this stem: **The good thing about pretending to dislike myself is—**

> *I beat other people to the punch.*
> *I have an excuse.*
> *no one expects things of me.*
> *people feel sorry for me.*
> *I don't have to do anything.*
> *it's easier.*
> *it's what my parents expect of me.*

If I had the courage to admit that, whatever my shortcomings, I like myself—

> *I'd be free.*
> *I'd be telling the truth.*
> *I'd have to separate from my family.*

I'd respect myself.
it'd be like stepping into another world.
everything would change.
the world would open to me.

I suggest you take your time and read these endings again. Don't rush past them. They reveal a good deal of valuable insight that may have relevance to you.

An attitude of self-acceptance is precisely what an effective psychotherapist strives to awaken in a person of even the lowest self-esteem. This attitude can inspire a person to face whatever he or she most dreads to encounter within, without collapsing into self-hatred, repudiating his or her value as a person, or surrendering the will to live. Thus, a person might be unhappy about experiencing poor self-esteem yet accept it along with the self-doubts and feelings of guilt—"I accept them as part of how I experience myself right now."

Sometimes people confuse the whole subject of self-esteem by declaring that everyone should have good self-esteem regardless of anything he or she does or fails to do. This is utterly impossible. They are confusing self-esteem, which necessarily depends on certain conditions, with self-acceptance, which can be unconditional.

Here is a simple sentence-completion exercise that will allow you to begin to explore the issue of self-acceptance in your own life.

Take a notebook and at the top of a page write the following stem: **Sometimes I dislike myself when I—** and then do six to ten endings as rapidly as you can. Once again, do not worry if your completions are all literally true. Don't censor yourself or you will learn nothing.

Then:

One of the things I dislike about myself is—
One of the things I like about myself is—
I like myself least when I—
I like myself most when I—
Mother gave me a view of myself as—
Father gave me a view of myself as—
When I feel disliked—
When I'm proud of something no one else cares about or understands—
If I were to admit how much I secretly like myself—
The good thing about pretending to dislike myself is—
The scary thing about admitting that, faults or no faults, I like myself is—
I am becoming aware—
If any of what I'm writing is true—
If I were willing to breathe deeply and allow myself to experience the joy of being—

There is a good chance that if you participate in this exercise fully and conscientiously, you will make contact with that part of yourself that is deeper than doubts, fears, and guilts. I hope so.

However, the discovery is not always greeted with delight. Sometimes it is frightening. Sometimes you want to pull back from it, refuse to accept it—because of some intuitive knowledge that to accept it fully is, almost irresistibly, to confront the responsibility of living consciously.

More than one client in therapy has protested, "If I accept the fact that I like myself, I'll have to behave differently!" Or, "If I accept the fact that I like myself, I'll have to stay too conscious!"

But when you fail to live consciously (and this is one of the most important facts about human psychology), the deepest and most primitive level of your being tends, in effect, to turn against you—by generating pain at the level of self-esteem. It is that deepest "I" we offend when we default on the integrity that positive self-esteem requires. If I do not have the loyalty to stand by a friend, that friend feels betrayed by me. By this token, if I do not have the loyalty to stand by myself (which means the courage to know that I like myself and to embrace the responsibility of doing so), then I, too, feel betrayed, even though I may be unable to explain my feeling or to articulate my experience.

If you review the material in this chapter, and the exercises you did, you will almost certainly be struck by the fact that you are more self-accepting in some areas than in others. You may accept certain of your physical attributes, thoughts, feelings, or actions, while denying or disowning others. Make a list of six facts about yourself you have difficulty accepting completely. This may require a challenging level of honesty from you. Remember that "accepting" does not mean "liking." Then, in your notebook, write **The hard thing about accepting** (fill in the item) **is**— and write six to ten endings. Then do the same for the stem **If I were to accept** (fill in the item) **completely**—. Then do **If it turns out that the truth is the truth whether I accept it or not**—. Then do **I am becoming aware**—.

Perhaps it is now clearer to you that self-acceptance is truly a heroic act.

What would it mean, practically, if over the next seven days you were to commit to experimenting each day with new instances of self-acceptance?

Chapter 5
Liberation from Guilt

Our goal is to have a strong, positive self-concept and to be able to maintain it regardless of our expertise or lack of it in any particular area, and regardless of the approval or disapproval of any other person.

In moving toward this goal, the way you think about your behavior (the standards by which you judge it and the context in which you see it) is vitally important—especially at times when you are inclined to condemn yourself. Guilt obviously subverts positive self-esteem.

Assessing your behavior entails certain questions like: By whose standards do you judge your behavior—your own or someone else's?

Do you seek to understand *why* you acted as you did? Do you consider circumstances, context, the options you perceived to be available at the time?

Do you assess your behavior as you would if it were exhibited by someone else?

When you think about your behavior, do you identify the specific areas or circumstances in which it occurs, or do you overgeneralize and say "I'm ignorant" when in fact you may be ignorant of a particular subject and quite knowledgeable about many other subjects, or say "I'm weak" when in fact you may lack courage or strength in a particular area and not in others?

If you regret your actions, do you attempt to learn from them, so that your future behavior does not repeat the same mistakes? Or do you merely suffer over the past and remain passively stuck in patterns of behavior you know to be inappropriate?

The answer to all these questions will have profound implications for your self-esteem.

We feel guilt when:
• contemplating something we have done or failed to do, we experience a diminished sense of self-worth

• we feel driven to rationalize or justify our behavior

• we feel defensive or combative when someone mentions the behavior

• we find it painfully difficult to remember or examine the behavior

Think of some action you have taken, or failed to take, for which you reproach yourself—something significant enough to have impacted your self-esteem. Then ask yourself: By *whose* standards am I judging? My own or someone else's? If the standards are not truly yours, then ask yourself: What do I *really* believe about this issue? If you are a thinking human being, and can honestly and with full consciousness see nothing wrong in your behavior, you may find the courage to stop condemning yourself right at this point. Or, at minimum, you may begin to gain a new perspective on the assessment of your behavior.

"I used to reproach myself," said Lucy, at one of our last therapy sessions, "because I have never wanted my mother to live with me—I mean, with me, my husband,

and our children. I was raised with the teaching that duty to one's parents comes ahead of everything. And that selfishness is a sin. But one of the things I got from therapy was to pay attention to what I *really* think, rather than what I sometimes tell myself I think. And the truth is that those teachings make no sense to me, especially in light of the fact that my mother always made it plain she didn't particularly like me and I know I don't particularly like her. We never got along. Her lifelong theme was gloom and doom. She used to tell me something was wrong with me if I was too happy. I looked at the fact that if I allowed my mother to live with us, it would have been hell for me and for my family. So I said no. Now my sisters and brothers don't speak to me. I see life differently than the rest of my family. And it's my life, not theirs. So I'll go by what seems rational to me, and I'll accept the consequences."

I am not suggesting that all values are subjective and that the moral is simply whatever an individual thinks or feels is moral. I develop my own concept of a rational and objective ethics—an ethics of rational or enlightened self-interest—in *Honoring the Self*. But people are often intimidated by the value preferences of others, at the expense of their own needs, perceptions, and self-esteem.

Further, I am not addressing the problems of psychopaths or people who appear to be lacking in normal guilt responses; if I were, I would have to touch on many issues I do not propose to cover here.

In the practice of therapy, much of the so-called guilt we encounter has to do with the disapproval or condemnation of significant others, such as parents or spouses; it is not always advisable to take (our own or anyone else's) declarations of guilt at face value. Often, when someone declares, "I feel guilty over such and such," what he or she really means but rarely acknowledges is, "I am afraid that if Mother or Father (or some other important person) knew what about what I had done, I would be criticized, repudiated, condemned." Often, the person does not actually regard the action as wrong, in which case what he or she feels is not literally guilt. So, the solution to this category of "guilt" is to *heed the authentic voice of the self*, to respect your own judgment above the beliefs of others that you do not genuinely share (though you may pretend to).

I recall therapy clients who professed to feel guilty over masturbation because when they were young their parents taught them it was sinful. Sometimes a therapist "solves" this problem by substituting his authority for that of the client's parents and assuring the client that masturbation is a perfectly acceptable activity. But this assumes that the "guilt" is caused by a mistaken idea about the morality of masturbation. I tend to regard this as the smokescreen problem. The deeper problem is dependency and fear of self-assertiveness; more specifically, fear of challenging the values of significant others. So I work first for a change of the definition of the problem as follows: *"I do not think masturbation is evil but I am afraid of the disapproval of my parents."* In thus reframing the problem, we have moved out of the arena of guilt and self-reproach; we have given the problem a more accurate and useful definition. And the challenge becomes: *Am I willing to stand by and act on my own perceptions and convictions?* Such willingness is one of the meanings of "honoring the self." As a person accepts this challenge, self-esteem rises.

Sometimes protestations of guilt are a smokescreen for denied and disowned feelings of resentment. Thus: "I have failed to live up to someone else's expectations or standards. I am afraid to admit that I am intimidated by those expectations and standards. I am afraid to ac-knowledge how angry I am over what is expected of me. So instead I tell myself and others that I feel guilty over failing to do what is right, and I do not have to fear that I will communicate my resentment and place my relation-ship with others in jeopardy."

If you recognize yourself in this description, the solution to your "guilt" is to be honest with yourself and others about your resentment. *First*, of course, you must be honest with yourself. Own your anger. Admit your resentment at standards and expectations not truly your own. And watch the "guilt" begin to disappear, although you may still have to work on your struggle for greater autonomy.

"If I weren't feeling guilty—" said Erwin in a sent-ence-completion exercise aimed at exploring just this issue, "I'd be feeling . . . agitated. If I weren't feeling guilty—I'd demand to know by what right my family expects me to support my bum of a brother. If I weren't feeling guilty—I'd demand to know why I'm expected to carry the problems of other people. If I weren't feeling guilty—I'd tell them I'm sick and tired of being responsible for a wimp who won't be responsible for himself. If I weren't feeling guilty—I'm *not* feeling guilty, *I'm feeling rage.*" And then: "If I were willing to be honest about my anger—I'd stop saying I feel guilty. If I were willing to be honest about my anger—I'd admit how different I am from the rest of my family. If I were willing to be honest about my anger—I'd feel cleaner and freer."

"If what I'm feeling is not really guilt—" said Eunice, an unhappily married woman in therapy, "I'll have to deal with my *resentment* of my husband's demands that I live only for him; I'll have to *face* that resentment. If what I'm feeling is not really guilt—I'd admit that I *love* being back at work again. If what I'm feeling is not really guilt—I'd scream about how tired I've been of sitting on my energy so my husband won't feel threatened."

Here again, the need for a change is seen in the definition of the problem. Undealt-with resentment and fear of self-assertion are the issues that have to be resolved, not guilt. The alleged guilt is merely a means of protecting oneself from this deeper challenge.

As you become more honest about your feelings, you give up the need to feel this kind of pseudo-guilt. And then you are freer to think clearly about values and expectations you may need to question and repudiate.

This task is by no means always an easy one. If it were, people would not hide behind pseudo-guilt. But if you are willing to make the effort, if you generate the courage to sustain the quest for independence (and you can), the benefit to your self-confidence and self-respect will be virtually immediate.

But let us suppose the standards *are* truly your own— and in some issue you have failed or betrayed them. You have undermined your sense of integrity.

As we emerge from childhood and develop our own values and standards, the maintenance of personal integrity assumes greater importance for our self-evaluation. *Integrity* means the integration of convictions, standards, beliefs, and behavior. When our behavior is congruent with our professed values, we have integrity.

Here is an exercise to facilitate your exploration of this issue. Write down these sentence stems in a notebook and do six to ten endings for each:

I most feel I have integrity when I—
Sometimes I diminish my integrity when I—

I like myself most when I—
I like myself least when I—
When I fail my standards I tell myself—
It would be easier for me to live up to my standards if—

Remember: If you get stuck, *invent*. Don't tell yourself you can't do it. You can. The only question is whether you choose to. When you have done the exercise, take a few minutes to meditate on your endings. What feelings arise for you? What do you become aware of? What have you learned? It would be helpful to make some notes at this point about what you've discovered about yourself.

When we behave in ways that conflict with our judgment of what is appropriate, we tend to lose face in our own eyes. We tend to respect ourselves less. But if we merely castigate ourselves, vilify ourselves, and think no more about it, we deteriorate our self-esteem *and increase the probability that we will have less integrity in the future.* A bad self-concept is a self-fulfilling prophecy: it leads to bad behavior. We do not improve by telling ourselves we are rotten. Our actions are a reflection of who and what we think we are. So we need to learn an alternative response to our defaults that will be more helpful to our self-esteem and to our future behavior.

Instead of collapsing into self-damnation, we can learn to ask: What were the circumstances? Why did my choices or decisions seem desirable or necessary in the context? What was I trying to accomplish? In what way was I trying to take care of myself?

We cannot understand a human being's actions until we understand why the actions make a kind of sense to the person involved. We need to know the *personal context* in which the actions occurred; we need to know the model of reality, the model of self-in-the-world, that lies behind the behavior.

For example: Suppose I am a woman who has chosen to remain too long with an alcoholic and physically abusive husband who is dangerous both to me and to my children. I know I should leave but I am afraid to. I see life as frightening, I see my situation as precarious, and I see my resources and options as extremely limited. Given my basic insecurity, my personal model of self-in-the-world, I *am trying to survive*, which is not a crime. I can wish I had more courage and confidence and did not suffer from so many anxieties, but I cannot damn myself for trying to live. I can only learn that better ways of living are possible, by changing my view of myself and the world.

Here is the important fact: If we can look at our personal context with compassion and the desire to understand (without for a moment denying the wrongness of our behavior); if we can be to ourselves a good friend who really wants to know where we were coming from when we behaved as we did—then we can heal ourselves; we can feel remorse and regret but not self-damnation. And the most likely consequence is the determination to do better in the future.

This, after all, is the pattern we encourage in therapy. A woman confesses a sexual infidelity; a man admits his perpetration of a rape; an employee acknowledges embezzling from his company; a teenager tells of willfully hurting a smaller sibling; a scientist admits to faking data; a parent confronts having been cruelly unmindful of a child's needs; a professor acknowledges taking credit for the work of a student; a secretary admits to calling in sick so as to have a date with her lover; a columnist confesses to maliciously fabricated gossip. Some of these actions may be minor, some calamitous in their consequences. But when our clients in therapy speak of them, and convey a sense of guilt, what do we do that is healing?

Typically, we say something like, "I see that you feel unhappy and self-reproachful about what you did. Let's try to understand why you did it. What were the feelings and considerations that prompted your behavior? Can we explore that?" (We do *not* hurl reproaches and we do *not* say, "What you did was right. There's nothing to feel bad about.")

You need to remember that, when you act, at some level you are always striving to satisfy your needs (as is true of all living organisms). Our actions are always related to our efforts to survive, or to protect the self, or to maintain equilibrium, or to avoid fear and pain, or to nurture ourselves, or to grow. Even if the path we choose is mistaken, even if *objectively* we are engaged in self-destruction, *subjectively* at some level we are trying to take care of ourselves—as in the case of a suicide who seeks escape from intolerable pain.

However, in seeking to understand the roots of undesirable behavior, there is no implication that the persons involved "couldn't help it." Neither understanding nor compassion entails denial of responsibility.

In fact, when a wrong has been committed over which a person feels guilt, I direct the client's attention to the question of what actions he or she might take to allow self-forgiveness. Let us examine this point, as it is important.

Self-forgiveness may require more than the understanding and compassion indicated above. Allowing for the fact that sometimes there are special circumstances requiring special considerations, there are, generally speaking, fairly specific steps we can take to free ourselves from guilt.

The first is to own (make real to ourselves, rather than deny or ignore) the fact that it is we who have taken the particular action.

The second, if another person has been harmed by our action, is to acknowledge explicitly to that person (or persons) the harm we have done and convey our understanding of the consequences of our behavior, assuming that this is possible.

The third is to take any and all actions available to us that might make amends or minimize the harm we have done (such as paying back stolen money, retracting a lie, and so on).

Finally, we need to make a firm commitment to behave differently in the future, *because without a change of behavior we will continually re-create self-distrust.*

Of course, there is also the step with which I started— the willingness to explore the reasons for our taking the action in the first place. If we evade that, we will not be free of guilt—and we will very likely repeat the pattern of inappropriate behavior.

Of course, some crimes are so terrible that self-forgiveness of the kind I am describing here is almost certainly unrealistic or impossible, such as, to name only a couple, the actions of a concentration-camp torturer or a mass-murderer. But such people are not known to seek psychotherapy or read books about self-esteem.

For those whom this discussion does concern, the evidence is overwhelming that if we can learn to understand and forgive ourselves, our behavior tends to improve. However, if we remain relentlessly self-condemning, our behavior (like our self-esteem) tends to worsen.

* * *

Here is an exercise to help you apply this principle. Write down, clearly and specifically, some action for which you reproach yourself. Explain *why* you consider your action wrong. Then close your eyes and imagine that it was not you but a friend you love who committed the action. Imagine interviewing your friend, drawing him or her out, helping this friend to articulate the model of self-in-the-world that was operative, guiding him or her to the perspective and feelings behind the behavior. Then imagine giving yourself this treatment. How does it make you feel? What do you become aware of? Record your experience in your notebook.

Then consider this: If you would feel it appropriate and desirable to give this benevolent perspective to someone you love, are you willing to give it to yourself?

Of course, if you would not give it to yourself, chances are you would not give it to anyone else, either. When we are irrationally harsh in judging our own behavior, we are usually no less harsh in judging other people's. Conversely, self-compassion, providing it is responsible and not merely self-indulgent, usually results in benevolence toward others. Benevolence, directed toward self and others, is both an expression of self-esteem and an enhancer of self-esteem.

Jerry consulted me about a number of personal problems, including a deep sense of guilt over having abandoned his wife and child when he had been married only a few years and his son was barely two. That was fifteen years ago, and while he had since divorced and remarried, he felt profoundly troubled by the damage he had done, particularly to his son. "How do I forgive myself?" he asked me. "How can I ever make it right?" I led him through the process just described, in which he imagined counseling a friend who had done what he had done, and he began to connect with the terror he had felt years ago, the sense of being overwhelmed by responsibilities beyond his power to meet, the knowledge that he did not love his wife and had merely succumbed to her pressure to marry out of an overdeveloped need to be perceived as "a good boy," and so on. He did not relinquish the conviction that he could have behaved more honorably and responsibly at the time, but he began to enter into the consciousness of his younger self and at least to appreciate that he had not been motivated by cruelty or capriciousness, and that in the universe as he had perceived it then he did not grasp the options that were evident to him now. He decided to find his son and former wife; acknowledge his error and his understanding of the pain he had caused; accept their right to heap any kind of anger on him they wished; and discover if there was anything he could do to assist them now. He forgave himself and he recognized their right not to forgive him if they did not choose to. He was free to see their pain with a clarity and compassion that was not possible as long as he was preoccupied with self-reproach—and, seeing it, he was able to move toward appropriate action. His wife had never remarried and he was unable to penetrate her wall of bitterness, but with his son he was able to establish a relationship that was deeply satisfying to them both, after a long and difficult period of suspiciousness, tears, and anger on the part of his son.

"Guilt and compassion just don't mix well," Jerry said to me. "So long as I was thinking about how rotten I was, another part of me was always feeling defensive and self-protective. When I let go of that, for the first time I could see their side of things in realistic terms. Now, whatever I can do for them, I am willing and happy to do. And that which I cannot do, I accept and make peace with."

One of the worst mistakes we can make is to tell ourselves that feeling guilty necessarily represents some kind of virtue. Intransigent harshness toward ourselves is nothing to boast about. It leaves us passive and powerless. It does not inspire change—it paralyzes. *Suffering* is just about the easiest of all human activities; *being happy* is just about the hardest. And happiness requires, not surrender to guilt, but emancipation from guilt.

Let us now consider another way in which we can harm our self-esteem by inappropriately assessing our behavior.

Sometimes we damage our self-esteem by generalizing about our "essential nature" on the basis of our actions in particular situations.

For example, Martin said to me, "I'm a social misfit. I'm no good at talking to people. I don't know what to say." When I asked, "Do you *never* know what to say?" he responded, "Well, no; when I'm with people who are interested in art or literature I have plenty to say." It seems that Martin had no particular interest in sports and felt inadequate when men and women at the office would discuss a recent football game. "Do you *care* about football?" I asked. He replied, "Not in the slightest." I went on, "Do you think you *should* care about football?" He reflected for a moment, then laughed and said, "No, of course not." I observed, "When you call yourself 'a social misfit,' what you seem to mean is that you have nothing to say about a subject that holds no interest for you and that you feel no desire to learn about. To me, that does not suggest an innate deficiency. It does suggest that you would be happier if you found some friends who share your interest in art and literature. As for your associates in the office, if you could give yourself permission to have interests different from theirs, and give them permission to have interests different from yours, I imagine you might feel more relaxed around them and might even discover that you're still members of the same species." As an aside to this story, future work with Martin disclosed that both he *and* his associates at work tended to move in unnecessarily restricted worlds, conversationally, and that plenty of potential avenues of communication existed between them in spite of their different interests.

"I'm a coward," said Chester. It seemed that Chester had a fear of public speaking. "What's the difference," I asked, "between saying 'I'm a coward' and saying 'I feel anxiety at the prospect of speaking in public'?" Chester responded, "Your version sort of cuts the problem down to size." I observed that everyone I knew who was self-confident in some situations was a good deal less so in others; and that if he wanted to learn confidence in public speaking, I thought he could do so easily; but that universalizing the problem to "cowardice" accomplished nothing but harm to his self-esteem.

"I'm terribly lazy," said Ed, who worked as an air-conditioner repair person and was often reproached by his boss for daydreaming on the job. But I learned that after his daytime job he worked well into the night on a thriller he was writing, which was the central passion of his life. All his life he had done everything but what he most wanted to do, and consequently he experienced almost constant frustration and self-dissatisfaction. But he was not "lazy." The bit of name-calling did nothing to move him closer to a solution but merely deteriorated his self-respect. "Suppose we say," I suggested, "that you find it terribly difficult to stay conscientiously disciplined about work that bores you, rather than that you're lazy. Now that's a problem, true enough, if you can't yet earn your living as a writer. But it's not the problem you've been attributing to yourself; you're not lazy when you're writing until three o'clock in the morning and then show up for your job in a fog. The real difficulty here is rough enough. Why make it worse with self-castigation?"

Now let us think about how you might apply this principle to yourself. Think of some negative attribute you ascribe to yourself. Then think of three situations in life where you do *not* exhibit it. Then see if you can think of any situations in which you actually manifest the *opposite* behavior (as with the case of Ed, who spent most of his time writing). Do this exercise—preferably making notes—with every negative trait you are inclined to attribute to yourself.

This gives you an opportunity to give up name-calling and assaults on your self-esteem and, further, to zero in on the *circumstances* in which you behave in ways you do not admire. Then try to identify the reasons why those situations seem to draw out this behavior.

The next step—and again, a notebook here is most useful—is to project three different alternative responses you might bring to those situations. Try out these new responses in your imagination. See which one you like best and that fits you best. Practice seeing yourself manifesting this new, more desirable behavior. See yourself performing your new behavior successfully; then go out and practice what you have rehearsed. It has been well established that this is a proven way to increase our efficacy in the world. If you persevere, even in the face of initial disappointments, setbacks, or "relapses," you will discover that you have radically underestimated your power to change (as almost everyone tends to do).

One of the characteristics of people who are reasonably free of guilt is not that they never take actions they regret or feel bad about, or even (for a time) reproach themselves for, but that, in addition to the corrective behaviors described above, they seek *to learn* from their mistakes. They reflect on them. They ponder them. They look for underlying patterns to identify—and to avoid.

Often, somewhere in our psyche we may "know" what we need to learn from our mistakes, but we do not "know" how to make our knowledge fully conscious. Here, sentence completion can be an immense help, since it is primarily a tool for gaining access to that which lies within us but beyond ordinary consciousness.

Thinking about some action (or inaction) for which you reproach yourself, write down this sentence stem: **If I were willing to look fully at what I did (or failed to do)—** then write six to ten endings as rapidly as possible, without interfering self-criticism or self-censorship, but, in effect, allowing the endings to write themselves (whether or not they initially seem to make sense). Then proceed with these sentence stems:

When I did what I did, I told myself—
One of the things I might learn from the experience is—
If I were willing to see what I see right now—
One of the ways to avoid this mistake in the future is—
If I were to remain as conscious as I am right now—
I would like myself more if I—
When I act against what I understand perfectly well—
I am becoming aware—

As I become more willing to understand what I am writing—
As I imagine how I would feel if I behaved more appropriately in the future—
As this issue becomes clearer and clearer to me—

There is no way to learn how healing and integrating this process can be except by your active participation in it. I will venture to guess that some readers will resist doing this process precisely because, at a subconscious level, they *know* the process has the power to activate growth and change—and if they are attached to their errors and to their guilt, change is not what they are seeking primarily, any protestations to the contrary notwithstanding.

Why would a person be attached to guilt? Well, for one thing, guilt leaves us locked in our passivity, with no need to generate new behaviors: "I'm guilty, I'm a disappointment, I always have been—such is life." This translates to: "Expect nothing of me."

For another, unhappiness is familiar; not enjoyable, but familiar. Who knows what life might confront us with if we didn't have our depression and our self-reproaches to insulate and protect us? Who knows what challenges we might then feel obliged to face? Misery can provide its own kind of coziness, whereas happiness, in its own way, is rather more demanding—in terms of consciousness, energy, discipline, dedication, and integrity.

Then there are the persons who were encouraged, when young, to believe that they were bad or inadequate, by unloving or unnurturing parents, and who, even as adults, feel driven to make their parents "right"—thus protecting the child-parent relationship—at the cost of their own fulfillment and self-esteem. This can go on long after our parents have died. The drama is *internal*.

So it takes courage to work at liberating ourselves from guilt. It takes honesty and perseverance and a commitment to independence—and to living consciously, authentically, responsibly, and actively. But it can be done.

This challenge confronts us not only in regard to our real or imagined shortcomings but in regard to our *assets*— if and when we are inclined to be defensive or self-reproachful about them.

When we condemn our thoughts, feelings, or actions, we do so, implicitly, to protect our self-esteem, even though the effect is directly opposite to what we intend. Since we are striving, at some level, to take care of or protect ourselves, our policy may have at least a surface plausibility. We are, after all, condemning that which we regard as flaws or shortcomings. But what about the rejection or repudiation of *positives*—even of *virtues*— within ourselves?

We have already seen an example of this, in our discussion of self-acceptance, when we noted that people may disown feelings of self-liking, or pride, through fear of the responsibility these feelings demand, or fear of imagined social alienation or the disapproval of others. But here are some other examples. Some readers will find it difficult to believe that anyone holds such views; others will recognize them too well.

"I feel guilty for being good-looking—that is, better-looking than most people."

Implication: My good looks are a reprimand—as well as an injustice—to all those who do not possess them.

Most likely translation: I am afraid of other people's jealousy or envy.

"I feel guilty for being so intelligent—that is, more intelligent than most people."

Implication: I was born with a good brain *at the expense of* all those who do not possess one. Furthermore, since everyone always chooses to exercise such potential intelligence as he or she is born with, I deserve no credit for what I have done with my endowment.

Most likely translation: I am afraid of the animosity of those who resent intelligence.

"I feel guilty over making a success of my life, when so many people fail to."

Implication: Not only do I deserve no moral credit for my achievements, but they represent an injustice against all those who, for whatever reason, did not achieve equally. Furthermore, I am in the moral debt of all those who have made less of their lives than I have of mine.

Most likely translation: If I do not give any indication of feeling proud of what I have accomplished, if I conceal my feelings of pride not only from others but from myself, then perhaps people will forgive me and like me.

"I feel guilty because I am human—I was born in sin."

Implication: It is meaningful to speak of guilt in a context where innocence does not exist. Furthermore, I must accept a concept that does violence to reason and morality because authorities proclaim it.

Most likely translation: Those authorities hold a monopoly on morality and moral judgments; who am I to set my judgment against theirs?

Two themes seem present wherever we encounter defensiveness or "guilt" about positives: fear of self-responsibility and fear of isolation or aloneness. Of course, the two are related. But it is unfortunate when persons are willing to belong *to* others in order to feel that they belong *with* them.

The desire for a sense of community is not, of course,

unreasonable, but to attempt to purchase it at the expense of self-esteem is merely to produce a new kind of loneliness: loneliness for ourselves. This is among the most common sources of human suffering.

If you feel touched by this issue, if you recognize any part of it in yourself, then I ask you to consider the following: If you had a child whom you loved, and that child was beautiful or healthy or strong or intelligent or creative—or grew up to be successful—*would you want your child to feel guilty about it?* Would you want your child to feel guilty over the fact of being *alive?* I put the issue this way because in my experience many people who are confused when thinking about themselves become instantly unconfused when they project their own psychology onto an imagined child.

Perhaps I should emphasize that to own and take pleasure in the best within ourselves is not to become arrogant, boastful, or grandiose; not at all. But neither should we be willing to lie—either to ourselves or to others—about who and what we are. We should not apologize to envy or seek to placate it. Healthy self-esteem forbids that kind of capitulation.

So we can see that courage may be required fully as much for honesty about our assets as about our shortcomings.

Here are some sentence stems to help you explore this issue:

If I have trouble accepting any asset of mine, it might be—
When I feel defensive about positives—
The scary thing about admitting my pride in myself or my accomplishments is—

When I encounter envy or jealousy—
If I hide who I am through fear of envy or jealousy—
If I am to judge myself sinful just because I exist—
If I am asked to apologize for my looks or intelli-
gence or possessions or achievements (circle and direct your completions to the item most pertinent to you)—
If I were willing to admit the things I feel pride about—

If you do this exercise in a notebook, writing half-a-dozen or so endings for each stem, I will hazard the guess that you do not need further explanations from me about the advantages of honestly accepting your assets, in terms of self-esteem (as well as happiness in general). The emotional rewards will be obvious and immediate.

Will you run the risk of alienating any person of low self-esteem who envies success or happiness? Almost inevitably. Does this mean that you may have to reassess some of your relationships? Probably. But as you learn to embrace your strengths, you will attract a new and better kind of relationship. That is a fact of life that, as a psychotherapist, I have witnessed many times. And in some cases you will redeem a present relationship—by inspiring another person to match your courage by rising to your level of honesty and authenticity. As one husband remarked to me, "My wife and I agreed to stop playing humble. What a relief."

The struggle for self-confidence and self-respect is worth what it asks of us.

There is one more related issue we need to address.

Our sense of self is not formed in a moment. It has a history. It develops over time. If our goal is to assess ourselves and our behavior appropriately, so as to clear the road to higher self-esteem, we often need to go into the past—to the self we were at an earlier point in our personal history—to reconnect with, embrace, and "forgive" our child-self or our teenage-self.

This is the subject to which we shall now turn.

Chapter 6
Integrating the Younger Self

"As a girl, I so desperately wanted my mother to love me," says a thirty-seven-year-old dentist. "I felt starved for simple touching or any kind of affection. Looking back, I'm appalled at how needy I seem to myself. I suppose that's why I don't like to look back. I don't like knowing that about myself, at least as I was then. Was that really me? I refuse to believe it. I like to think that girl died a long time ago and I'm somebody else."

When her husband leaves her, complaining that she seems incapable of either giving or receiving love, she is devastated and bewildered; she professes not to understand what he means.

"I don't like to remember myself as a young child," echoes a forty-six-year-old male computer programmer. "I was so terrified all the time. My father coming home drunk—hitting whoever came within his reach. Mother never protecting us. Me hiding; looking for places to hide; too scared half the time even to talk. It was sickening; that child was sickening. I don't feel any connection to him."

His children do not understand why Daddy seems

incapable of playing with them. They know only that, emotionally, Daddy rarely seems there—as if they have no father.

"Mother was so sarcastic," says a thirty-one-year-old female nurse. "She had a tongue that could kill. When I was a small child, I couldn't handle that. I cried so much. I cringe when I think of myself at age three, four, five."

But any number of her patients have complained about her brusque manner and her occasional biting remarks. She knows she tends to be disliked but is mystified as to why.

"When I was twelve," says a fifty-one-year-old male lawyer, "there was a bully on our block who terrified me. He beat me up a few times, and after that, just seeing him, I would feel reduced to nothing. I don't like to remember that. I don't like to talk about it. In fact, I don't like to admit that frightened little boy was me. Why couldn't he handle the situation better? I'd just as soon forget about the little bastard."

Although he is brilliant in his work, few of his clients are able to like him. They perceive him as insensitive and cruel. "He's a bully," more than one client has remarked.

There are many reasons why people feel that they cannot forgive the child they once were. Like the clients quoted above, they deny and disown that child. Translated into words, their attitude amounts to the following: I cannot forgive that I was so frightened by my mother; that I so desperately craved my father's approval; that I felt so unlovable; that I so hungered for attention and affection; that I was so confused by things; that I somehow sexually aroused my mother; that I did something, even if I have no idea what, to make my father molest me; that I was so awkward in gym class; that I was so intimidated by my teacher; that I hurt so much; that I wasn't popular at school; that I was timid; that I was shy; that I wasn't tougher; that I was afraid to disobey my parents; that I would do anything to be liked; that I was starved for kindness; that I was angry and hostile; that I was jealous of my younger brother; that I felt everyone understood more than I did; that I didn't know what to do when I was being ridiculed; that I didn't stand up to people; that my clothes were always the poorest and shabbiest of anyone's at school.

In effect, the child we once were can be experienced as a source of pain, rage, fear, embarrassment, or humiliation, to be repressed, disowned, repudiated, forgotten. We *reject* that child just as, perhaps, *others once did*—and our cruelty to that child can continue daily and indefinitely through our lifetime, in the theater of our own psyche where the child continues to exist as a subpersonality, a *child-self*.

Unaware of what we are doing, we may, as adults, profess to find evidence of being rejected everywhere in our current relationships, not realizing that the roots of our experience of rejection are internal rather than external. Our whole lives can be acts of nonstop self-repudiation, while we go on complaining that others do not love us.

When we learn to forgive the child we once were for what he or she didn't know, or couldn't do, or couldn't cope with, or felt or didn't feel; when we understand and accept that that child was struggling to survive the best way he or she could—then the adult-self is no longer in an adversarial relationship to the child-self. One part is not at war with another part. Our adult responses are more appropriate.

In chapter 2 I introduced the concept of a child-self—

the internal representation of the child we once were, the constellation of attitudes, feelings, values, and perspectives that were ours long ago, and that enjoys psychological immortality as a component of our total self. It is a *sub*self, a *sub*personality—a mind state that can be more or less dominant at any given time, and out of which we sometimes operate quite exclusively without necessarily being aware of doing so.

We can (implicitly) relate to our child-self consciously or unconsciously, benevolently or with hostility, compassionately or harshly. As I trust the exercises in this chapter will make clear, when related to consciously and positively a child-self can be assimilated and integrated into the total self. When related to unconsciously and/or negatively, a child-self is left in a kind of alienated oblivion. In the latter case, when the child-self is left unconscious, or is disowned and repudiated, we are fragmented; we do not feel whole; in some measure we feel self-alienated; and self-esteem is wounded.

Left unrecognized, not understood, or rejected and abandoned, a child-self can turn into a "troublemaker" that obstructs our evolution as well as our enjoyment of existence. The external expression of this phenomenon is that we will at times exhibit harmfully childish behavior, or fall into patterns of inappropriate dependency, or become narcissistic, or experience the world as belonging to "the grown-ups."

On the other hand, recognized, accepted, embraced, and thereby integrated, a child-self can be a magnificent resource that enriches our lives, with its potential for spontaneity, playfulness, and imaginativeness.

Before you can befriend and integrate a child-self, so that it exists in harmonious relationship to the rest of you, you must first make contact with that entity within your inner world. By way of introducing clients or students to their child-selves, I sometimes ask them to enter a fantasy, to imagine themselves walking along a country road and, in the distance, to see a small child sitting by a tree and, as they draw near, to see that that child is the self they once were. Then I ask them to sit down by the tree and enter into dialogue with the child. They are encouraged to speak aloud, to deepen the reality of the experience. What do they want and need to say to each other? Not uncommonly there are tears; sometimes there is joy. But there is almost always the realization that in some form the child still exists within the psyche (as a mind state) and has a contribution to make to the life of the adult—and a richer, fuller self emerges from the discovery. Often, there is the sad realization that they had mistakenly thought they needed to rid themselves of that child in order to grow up.

When working with a client toward the goal of integrating a child-self, I will often suggest this simple exercise that you can easily do yourself. (If you have a friend who can read the following instructions to you, so much the better; or you can read them into a cassette recorder and then play them back; or simply read them until you master them before proceeding.)

Spend a few minutes looking at photographs of yourself as a young child (assuming you have some; otherwise, proceed without them). Then close your eyes and take several deep, relaxing breaths. Go inside and explore these questions: What did it feel like to be five years old? How do you imagine you experienced your body then? . . . What did it feel like to be sad? . . . What did it feel like to be excited? . . . What was it like living in your home? . . . How did you sit? Sit as you *imagine* a five-year-old sits. Pay attention to what you are feeling. Stay with the experience.

If you did nothing else but this one exercise every day for two or three weeks, you would begin to achieve not only an enhanced awareness of your child-self but also a higher level of integration than you probably experience at present—because you would be taking the first step toward making the child-self *visible* and treating him or her *seriously*.

But sentence-completion work is a more advanced and powerful tool for awakening your awareness of your child-self and facilitating integration. As I've mentioned before, use a notebook, and write each of the incomplete sentences listed below at the top of a fresh page, then write six to ten endings for each, working as rapidly and as unself-critically as you can, *inventing* when need be to keep the momentum going.

When I was five years old—
When I was ten years old—
If I recall how the world seemed when I was very young—
If I recall how my body felt when I was very young—
If I recall how people seemed when I was very young—
With my friends I felt—
When I felt lonely I—
When I felt excited I—
If I recall how life seemed when I was very young—
If the child in me could speak, he/she might say—
One of things I had to do as a child to survive was—
One of the ways I treat my child-self as my mother did is—
One of the ways I treat my child-self as my father did is—
When the child within feels ignored by me—

When the child within feels criticized by me—
One of the ways that child sometimes gets me into
trouble is—
I suspect I am operating out of my child-self when
I—
If that child were to feel accepted by me—
Sometimes, the hard thing about fully accepting the
child within is—
If I were more forgiving of my child-self—
I would be kinder to the child within if I were to—
If I were to listen to the things that child needs to tell
me—
If I fully accept that child as a valuable part of me—
I am becoming aware—
When I look at myself from this perspective—

I have had clients do this exercise several times, at intervals of about a month. They were asked not to look at how they ended the stems on previous occasions. Each time they generated some new endings that took them deeper. With no other work in this area they achieved extraordinary insights and integrations that resulted in self-healing and enhanced self-esteem.

I recommend that you experiment with this set of sentence completions and discover what it can accomplish for you. In doing this, it will become more real to you how such work can benefit your self-confidence, self-respect, and sense of wholeness.

Here is a more advanced way to work on the territory opened up in the above sentence stems. Do again the stem **When I was five years old—** followed by **One of the things my five-year-old-self needs from me and has never gotten is—** followed by **When my five-year-old-self tries to talk to me—** followed by **If I were willing to listen to** my **five-year-old-self with acceptance and compassion—** followed by **If I refuse to be there for my five-year-old-self**— followed by **At the thought of reaching back to help my five-year-old-self—**. Then do this same set for your six-, seven-, eight-, nine-, ten-, eleven-, and twelve-year-old selves. You will perform a miracle of self-healing.

Finally, when you feel you have established a good sense of your child-self as a psychological entity, which the sentence-completion work should give you, here is one more exercise to facilitate integration that is both simple and extraordinarily powerful.

Using whatever kind of imagery works for you—sight, hearing, kinesthetic feelings—generate the sense of your child-self standing in front of you (as I asked Charles to do in chapter 2). Then, without saying a word, imagine holding that child in your arms, embracing and gently stroking, so that you are in a nurturing relationship to him or her. Allow the child to respond or not to respond. Remain gentle and firm. Let the touch of your hands, your arms, and your chest communicate acceptance, compassion, respect.

I recall a client, Charlotte, who initially had difficulty with this exercise because, she said, her child-self was an amalgam of pain, rage, and suspiciousness. "She keeps slipping away," Charlotte said. "She doesn't trust me—or anybody." I pointed out that, given little Charlotte's experiences, her response was perfectly natural. Then I went on, "Imagine that I came to you with a little girl and said, 'Here is someone I would like you to take care of. She's had some pretty bad experiences and is very distrustful of people. For one thing, an uncle attempted to molest her, and when she tried to tell her mother, her mother became angry at her. So she feels abandoned and betrayed. [Charlotte had had this experience at the age of six.] Her new home—and her new life—will be with you. You will have to help her learn to trust you and to realize that you are different from the other grown-ups she's encountered.' Later, you can talk to her—and listen, and let her tell you all the things she needs an adult to understand. But first, just hold her. Let her feel safety through the quality of your being, the quality of your presence. Can you do that?"

"Yes," Charlotte replied eagerly. "Up till now, I've been treating her like everyone else has. Pretending she didn't exist, wasn't there, because her pain frightened me. I think I've been blaming her, too, *almost as my mother did.*"

"Then close your eyes, create her in front of you, then take her in your arms and allow her to feel your nurturing. And what is that like for you? . . . And I wonder what you might like to say to her. . . . Take your time and explore that."

Later, Charlotte remarked, "All these years I've tried to be an adult by denying the child I once was. I was so ashamed and hurt and angry. But I truly felt like an adult for the first time when I took her in my arms and accepted her as part of me."

This is one of the ways we build self-esteem.

Now let us consider the teenage-self.

Each of us was once a teenager, and we still carry that teenager with us, as part of who we are, whether we recognize that younger entity or not. If we recognize, accept, and befriend our teenage-self, it can be an invaluable resource of energy, idealism, ambition, and provide an unlimited sense of life's possibilities. But if repudiated, ignored, disowned, or denied, our teenage-self can lead us to many kinds of self-sabotaging behavior. We may find ourself talking back to the boss in the wrong way and at the wrong moment, or viewing the opposite sex with a teenager's fear and uncertainty, or acting with a teenager's (occasional) lack of good critical judgment, or turning any older person into a repressive, authoritative parent-figure against whom we feel the need to rebel.

But, beyond all that, if we leave our teenage-self alienated from our total self, we allow a fissure to exist within us, a split in our identity that affects self-esteem adversely. Once again, one part of us is at war with another part.

We can observe that kind of war in the following statements.

"It's embarrassing to remember how shy and awkward I was with girls during my adolescent years," said a middle-aged physician. "Really, who wants to think about such things? What has that poor character got to do with me?"

So his teenage-self is left to wait for *someone* who will not perceive him as a "character"; the one person who could save him does not want the disgrace of associating with him. And the adult struggles not to think about the inexplicable moments of vague, haunting loneliness that hit him at unpredictable times, from a source he cannot imagine.

"I still wanted to have my family take care of me when I was approaching eighteen," said a forty-one-year-old wife and mother, "while another part of me dreamed of being free and on my own. I wasn't very independent. No guts, I suppose. What's the big deal about going out on your own? But I was rebelling one minute and crawling back into the nest a minute later. Looking back, it all seems so weak. I have no tolerance for indecision. I can't relate to that teenage girl at all. Do you suppose that's why I'm often so impatient with my own teenage daughters? I have trouble relating to them, too."

So her teenage-self—and her teenage daughters—are left without the understanding, compassion, and support of the very person from whom they need it most. And the adult struggles to keep busy so as not to feel the echoes of a distant, bewildering pain that time fails to heal.

"I hate remembering how lonely I was during my high school years," said a forty-eight-year-old mechanic. "I wasn't good with people, yet I was dying for someone to talk to! I was so . . . intense. Awful. Why do you psychologists like dragging up the past? As a teenager, I was a creep."

So his teenage-self is sentenced to immutable loneliness. And the adult is left to wonder about a mystifying void within himself that nothing will fill.

Once again we can observe the pattern of uncompassionate, unempathic harshness—this time directed at the self of our adolescent years. Thus: I cannot forgive my social awkwardness as a teenager; I cannot forgive my fear of girls/boys; or my painful longing for someone to be with and talk to; or the enormous confusion I felt about almost everything; or my incompetence at athletics and at dancing; or my gangliness; or my complexion; or my noisy boisterousness; or my confusions about sex; or my vacillations between rebelliousness and compliance; or my shyness at parties; or my passivity; or my bouts with delinquency; or my promiscuity; or my puritanism; or my exhibitionism; or my grandiosity; or my timidity; or my lack of knowledge, or poise, or sophistication.

Just as we can reject the child we once were, so we can reject the teenager. But our teenage-self remains an enduring component of our psyche, and our only choice is whether we will be conscious or unconscious of that subself, benevolent and empathic or hostile and condemning. Will our teenage-self be accepted and embraced—made to feel welcome, in effect—or sentenced to the lifelong role of a lonely outcast?

Let us turn to the same exercise I introduced to make contact with the child-self, now adapted for the adolescent years.

If possible, begin by spending a few minutes looking at photographs of yourself taken when you were a teenager. Then close your eyes and take several deep, relaxing breaths. Go inside and explore the questions: What does it feel like to be a teenager? . . . How do you imagine you experienced your body then? . . . What was it like living in your home? . . . How did you sit? Sit as you *imagine* a teenager sits. Pay attention to what you are feeling. Stay with the experience. Slowly, a richer perspective on who you are will open to you. Greet it with acceptance and respect.

This is another simple exercise you will find beneficial to repeat on a daily basis for two or three weeks (after you have completed your work with the child-self). You will find that, as you give your teenage-self understanding and respect, you feel more whole, more integrated, and more inwardly harmonious.

Next, let us turn to sentence completion as a means of carrying this work further. Write each of the following stems on the top of a separate page in your notebook, then write six to ten endings for each stem.

When I became a teenager—
When I was fourteen years old—
When I was sixteen years old—
When I entered high school I felt—

With my teenage friends I felt—
With the opposite sex I felt—
As a teenager, one of the things I had to do to survive was—
As a teenager, when I felt angry I—
As a teenager, when I felt pain I—
As a teenager, when I felt fear I—
As a teenager, when I felt lonely I—
As a teenager, when I felt excited I—
When I was eighteen years old—
If the teenager in me could speak, he/she might say—
One of the ways I treat my teenage-self as my mother did is—
One of the ways I treat my teenage-self as my father did is—
When my teenage-self feels ignored by me—
When my teenage-self feels criticized by me—
One of the ways my teenage-self sometimes gets me into trouble is—
If my teenage-self felt listened to and respected by me—
If my teenage-self felt I had compassion for his/her struggles—
Sometimes, the hard thing about fully accepting the teenager within is—
If I were more forgiving of my teenage-self—
If I were responsive to the teenager's needs—
One of the ways my teenage-self could contribute to my life is—
One of the things I appreciate about my teenage-self is—
I am beginning to suspect—
If I allow myself to understand what I have been writing—

Working with this process in therapy, I have observed that some clients resist the work angrily, because, they say, they were such confused, lonely, mixed-up teenagers that they literally want nothing to do with that entity. They forget that that entity now resides within them and that it is *themselves* they are repudiating.

Some of the above sentence stems are aimed at resolving this issue. For instance, when doing the stem **When my teenage-self feels ignored by me**— they produce such endings (to their surprise) as: he acts up; she becomes spiteful; he gets me to do stupid things; she becomes foolishly defiant; he makes me confused; she makes me act half my age; he makes me reckless; she makes me irresponsible; and so on. Then, when doing such stems as **If I were more forgiving of my teenage-self**— or **If I were responsive to the teenager's needs**— they produce such endings as: he would melt; she would be less suspicious; he would help me rather than fight me; she would feel a part of me; he would allow me to use my knowledge; she wouldn't get me involved in things I should keep away from; he wouldn't be so rebellious; she wouldn't be so sullen; and so on.

These endings speak for themselves. When we declare war on ourselves, we create an adversary we cannot conquer. When we accept and respect, we create a friend and ally.

As I did with the child-self, I want to give some more advanced stems for the teenage-self. Begin with the stem **When I was thirteen years old**— and follow this with **One of the things my thirteen-year-old-self needs from me and has never gotten is**— and then **When my thirteen-year-old-self tries to talk to me**— and then **If I were willing to listen to my thirteen-year-old-self with acceptance and compassion**— and then **If I refuse to be there for my**

thirteen-year-old-self— and finally **At the thought of reaching back to help my thirteen-year-old-self—**. Then do the same for each of your "selves" up to age nineteen (and even beyond if you really wish to be ambitious). You will feel more whole, more integrated than you have ever felt before in your life.

And then remember the fourth exercise proposed for integrating the child-self—and adapt it to the teenage-self. Use your imagination to place that self in front of you. What do you two imagine you might feel, looking at each other? And if you were to reach out your arms in a gesture of affection and trust, what might that feel like? And if you were to embrace that self (as one embraces a teenager, not a child)—communicating not with words but with your hands, arms, and body—sending messages of compassion and nurturing—what might your experience be? Do it— and find out. Pay attention to the full range of your feelings. Persevere, regardless of what response you receive from your teenage-self. In healing the teenager, you heal yourself.

I know that such an exercise will appear strange to many readers. Alone in your room—creating a relationship of nurturing to the adolescent you once were? What has that got to do with how you feel about yourself today? If you do the exercise—not once, perhaps, but several times—you will discover the answer.

The exercise need take only two or three minutes. And yet, persevered in daily for a month or two, you will notice a difference in your experience of yourself. A war in which you have been engaging—unconsciously—for years will end. If you keep a journal during this period, and every few days write half-a-dozen endings for the stem **I am beginning to feel—** you will have a clearer sense of your progress.

The mere commitment to do this exercise, as well as the preceding ones, enhances your self-esteem, because the implication is that you consider yourself worthy of this kind of effort. When and if you find yourself reluctant to make the effort, perhaps the question you need to consider is: *What have I got to do that is more important?*

Chapter 7
Living Responsibly

Men and women who enjoy high self-esteem have an *active* orientation to life rather than a *passive* one. They take full responsibility for the attainment of their desires. They do not wait for others to fulfill their dreams.

If there is a problem, they ask, "What can I do about it? What avenues of action are possible to me?" They do not cry, "Someone's got to do something!" If something has gone wrong, they ask, "What did I overlook? Where did I miscalculate?" They do not indulge in orgies of blame.

In short, they take responsibility for their own existence.

And by the principle of reciprocal causation discussed earlier (acts that are causes of good self-esteem are also expressions of good self-esteem), people who take responsibility for their own existence tend thereby to *generate* healthy self-esteem. To the extent that we shift from a passive to an active orientation, we like ourselves more, trust ourselves more, and feel more competent to live and more deserving of happiness.

Working with clients in psychotherapy, I often see that the most radical transformation occurs after the client's realization that no one is coming to the rescue. "No one is coming" is a constant theme of my work on every possible level. "When I finally allowed myself to face full responsibility for my life," more than one client has said to me, "I began to grow. I began to change. And my self-esteem began to rise."

Self-responsibility entails such realizations as the following:

I am responsible for my choices and actions.

I am responsible for the way I prioritize my time.

I am responsible for the level of consciousness I bring to my work.

I am responsible for the care or lack of care with which I treat my body.

I am responsible for being in the relationships I choose to enter or to remain in.

I am responsible for the way I treat other people—my spouse, my children, my parents, my friends, my associates, my boss, my subordinates, the salesclerk in a department store.

I am responsible for the meaning I give or fail to give to my existence.

I am responsible for my happiness.

I am responsible for my life—materially, emotionally, intellectually, spiritually.

When I speak of "being responsible" in this context, I mean responsible not as the recipient of moral blame or guilt, but responsible as the chief causal agent in your life and behavior. This is an important point.

In discussing some of the applications of self-responsibility in *Honoring the Self*, I wrote:

. . . a client in therapy learns to question, "Why and how do I make myself so passive?" rather than bemoaning, "Why am I so passive?" Instead of asserting that he can't care about anything, the client learns to explore why and how he prevents himself from experiencing strong feelings about anything. "Why," in this context, means, "For what purpose?" Instead of saying, "Why does the back of my neck become painfully tense?" the client learns to say, "What feelings am I trying to avoid experiencing by tensing my neck muscles?" Instead of complaining that people are so often taking advantage of her, the client learns to say, "Why and how do I invite or encourage people to take advantage of me?" Instead of complaining, "No one understands me," the client asks, "Why and how do I make it difficult for people to understand me?" Instead of saying, "Why do women always turn away from me?" the client confronts the question, "Why and how do I cause women to turn away from me?" Instead of moaning, "I always fail at whatever I attempt," the client begins to consider, "Why and how do I always cause myself to fail at whatever I attempt?"

I am far from suggesting that a person never suffers through accident or through the fault of others, or that a person is responsible for everything that may happen to him or her. We are not omnipotent. I do not support the grandiose notion that "I am responsible for every aspect of my existence and everything that befalls me."

Some things we have control over; others we do not. If I hold myself responsible for matters beyond my control, I will put my self-esteem in jeopardy since inevitably I will fail my own expectations. If I deny responsibility for matters that are within my control, again I will jeopardize my self-esteem. I need to know the difference between that which is and is not up to me. I also need to know that I am responsible for my attitude and actions regarding those things I do not have control over, such as the behavior of other people.

Self-responsibility, rationally conceived, is indispensable to good self-esteem. Avoiding self-responsibility victimizes us with regard to our own lives. It leaves us helpless. We give power to everyone except ourselves. When we are frustrated, we look for someone to blame; *others* are at fault for our unhappiness. By contrast, the appreciation of self-responsibility can be an exhilarating and empowering experience. It places our lives back in our own hands.

Sentence completion brings the point home with speed and clarity.

"If I were to give up blaming my wife for my unhappiness—" said a middle-aged real estate broker, "I'd have to confront my own passivity; I'd have to face the fact that I've been sad most of my life; I'd have to recognize that I choose to remain with her when no one forces me to; I'd have to admit that I need someone to blame; I'd be giving up my control over her; I'd have to look at my options; *I'd have to do something other than just suffer.*"

"If I were to accept that I am responsible for the condition of my body—" said a young woman who ate and drank too much, "I'd have to give up feeling sorry for myself; I'd have to stop blaming my parents for everything; I'd probably have to start exercising; I don't think I could go on abusing my body as I do now; I'd like myself more; I'd get in shape; I'd stop wallowing in self-pity; I'd get off my butt and *do something about it."*

"If I took responsibility for my feelings—" said a wife and mother whose emotional eruptions were a nonstop storm through the lives of her family, "I'd have to look at the fact that when I'm frustrated I become like a child; I'd have to face up to what I'm really unhappy about; I'd know that a lot of my anger is a cover-up for insecurity; maybe I could be more honest with my husband about my fears; I wouldn't torment the kids; I'd have to admit that often I use emotions to manipulate my family into doing what I want; I'd have to accept that other people have feelings; I'd think before I spoke; *I wouldn't see myself as a victim of the universe."*

"If I took responsibility for getting what I want—" said a man in his thirties who had never held a job for longer than eight months, "I'd have to recognize that time is going by; I'd face that I'm not getting any younger; I wouldn't daydream and fantasize so much; I'd have to admit that all I've ever done is spin my wheels; I'd have to admit how scared I am of really committing myself to anything; I wouldn't envy other people's success so much; I couldn't keep blaming the system; I'd settle into one direction and stay with it; I'd stop coming up with alibis; *I'd recognize that nothing is going to get better unless I change."*

"So long as I can blame my parents for my unhappiness—" said a thirty-four-year-old schoolteacher who switched therapists several times a year, "I never have to grow up; I can get people to feel sorry for me; I can make my folks feel guilty; I can make other people feel they've got to make it up to me; I can tell myself it's not my fault; I can defeat my therapists; I can feel tragic; I can be a victim; I have an excuse for everything; *I don't have to take charge of my life."*

"If I were to take full responsibility for my own life—" said a psychiatrist who was responsive to everyone's needs except his own or his family's, "I'd stop telling myself I'm too busy to be happy; I'd stop trying to impress my patients with how kind and compassionate I am; I'd stop feeling like a martyr; I'd stop insisting that my wife has to make unlimited allowances for me; I'd know where my responsibility to others stops; I'd be kinder to myself and kinder to my wife and kids; I'd recognize that self-sacrifice is a cop-out; I'd start applying to myself what I teach my patients; I'd admit that no one can live for others and shouldn't if they could; I'd live with more integrity; I'd respect myself more and so would my family; *I'd have to think about what I really want in life.*"

If you have not yet done the sentence-completion exercises in this book, you may be astonished at the candor with which people acknowledge the pay-offs of avoiding self-responsibility. But if you truly want to raise your self-esteem, here are some sentence stems to work with before proceeding further:

> **Sometimes, when things aren't going well, I make myself helpless by—**
> **The good thing about making myself helpless is—**
> **Sometimes I try to avoid responsibility by blaming—**
> **Sometimes I keep myself passive by—**
> **Sometimes I use self-blame to—**
> **If I took more responsibility when working—**
> **If I took more responsibility for the success of my relationships—**
> **If I took responsibility for every word I utter—**
> **If I took responsibility for my feelings—**
> **If I took responsibility for my actions, moment by moment—**

If I took responsibility for my happiness—
If the only meaning in my life is the meaning I am
willing to create—
If I were willing to breathe deeply and fully experi-
ence my own power—
If I were willing to see what I see and know what I
know—
Right now it is very clear that—

Perhaps you are aware that in some areas of your life you are less self-responsible than in others. You may be very active and responsible at work and very passive at home with your family. You may be very responsible about your health and very irresponsible about money. You may be active about your intellectual development and passive about your emotions.

Consider the following areas:

Your health
Your emotions
Your choice of lovers
Your choice of spouse
Your choice of friends
Your financial well-being
The level of consciousness and responsibility you bring to your work
The level of consciousness and responsibility you bring to your relationships
Your way of treating people in general
Your intellectual development
Your character
Your happiness
Your self-esteem

Now imagine a scale from 1 to 10, with 10 signifying what you would regard as optimal self-responsibility and 1 signifying the lowest conceivable level of self-responsibility. Rate yourself on each item by putting a number beside it. You can isolate the areas most in need of work.

At this point, if you think about one or another of the areas where you are not very responsible, you may find yourself protesting, "But I don't know what to *do*—I don't know *how* to be more responsible."

Of course, this is rarely true.

In my early practice, when clients would raise this objection, I would actually show and tell them what they could do to become more active participants in their own lives. Experience has taught me the fallacy of this approach. Today, after clients know how to do sentence completion, I usually give them the stem **One of the ways I can take more responsibility with regard to** (fill in the area) **is to—** and tell them to proceed full speed ahead. Then they begin to appreciate how knowledgeable they really are.

I have heard many people, from all backgrounds and walks of life, produce stunningly insightful endings for this stem, and I have learned to listen with benevolent skepticism to protestations of ignorance and helplessness. If you hear yourself protesting, I suggest you do the same.

Of course, sometimes other people can help us to become more aware of some action possibilities, but there are always some things we already know we can do. *Begin with these.*

To accept responsibility for one's existence is to recognize the need to live productively. This is a basic and profoundly important application of the idea of having an active orientation to life.

It is not the degree of our productive ability that is at issue here, but rather our choice to exercise whatever ability we do possess. Productive work is the supremely *human* act. Animals must adjust themselves to their physical environment; human beings adjust the physical environment to themselves. We have the capacity to give psychological and existential unity to our lives by integrating our actions with goals projected across our lifetimes.

It is not the kind of work we select that affects our self-esteem (provided, of course, that the work is not inimical to human life), but whether we seek work that requires and expresses the fullest, most conscientious use of our minds and values (assuming that the opportunity to do so exists).

To live productively is to provide ourselves with one of the unique joys and rewards of being human.

Living responsibly (and thereby fostering healthy self-esteem) is intimately associated with living actively. It is through actions that an attitude of self-responsibility is implemented and expressed. What *actions* can I take that will bring me closer to my goals? What *actions* can I take to advance my career?—to improve my love life?—to elicit better treatment from others?—to raise my income?—to make myself happier?—to cultivate my intellectual or spiritual development?

Just as, if we wish to raise our self-esteem, we need to think in terms of *behaviors*, if we wish to live more responsibly, we need to think in very specific *action* terms. For example, it is not good enough to tell yourself, "I should be more conscientious." What will you *do* if you are more conscientious? It is not good enough to say, "I should have a better attitude with my family." How will a better attitude be manifested in specific *behavior*?

Behavior can be mental or physical. Thinking is an action; holding your focus on the task to be done is an action; making a list is an action; making a statement to another person is an action; and so is caressing a face, conveying appreciation in words, writing a letter, acknowledging a mistake, preparing a report, balancing a checkbook, or applying for a job. The question is always: Is the behavior appropriate to the context? To be self-responsible is to be concerned with that question.

Therefore, if we want to practice greater self-responsibility in some aspect of our lives, we need to consider: What actions are possible to me here? What are my options? If I am not waiting for a miracle, or for someone else to *do something*, then what can *I* do? If I choose to do nothing, to accept the status quo, am I willing to take responsibility for that decision?

Observe this: If there are areas of your life in which you practice a higher level of self-responsibility than you do in others, my guess is that those are also the areas in which *you like yourself most*. The areas in which you most avoid responsibility are the areas in which you like yourself least.

Once again, I recommend sentence completion to check this out. Thus: **I practice greatest self-responsibility when I—; I most avoid self-responsibility when I—; When I am self-responsible I feel—; When I avoid self-responsibility I feel—; If any of what I am writing is true—; I am becoming aware—.**

Once again, think about the next seven days of your life. If you were to practice greater self-responsibility, what might you do differently? Write your answer in a notebook.

Then consider translating what you have written into

action. Don't think of committing yourself for a lifetime, just for the next seven days—as an experiment. Discover the impact on your sense of self. Discover the impact on your life.

Then, if you like what you discover, try seven more days. Then seven more.

Chapter 8
Living Authentically

The lies most devastating to our self-esteem are not so much the lies we *tell* as the lies we *live*.

We live a lie when we misrepresent the reality of our experience or the truth of our being.

Thus I am living a lie when I pretend a love I do not feel; when I pretend an indifference I do not feel; when I present myself as more than I am; when I present myself as less than I am; when I say I am angry and the truth is I am afraid; when I pretend to be helpless and the truth is I am manipulative; when I deny and conceal my excitement about life; when I affect a blindness that denies my awareness; when I affect a knowledgeability I do not possess; when I laugh when I need to cry; when I spend unnecessary stretches of time with people I dislike; when I present myself as the embodiment of values I do not feel or hold; when I am kind to everyone except the persons I profess to love; when I fake beliefs to win acceptance; when I fake modesty; when I fake arrogance; when I allow my silence to imply agreement with convictions I do not share; when I profess to admire one kind of person while consistently sleeping with another.

Good self-esteem demands *congruence* —which means

that the self within and the self manifested in the world be in accord.

If I choose to fake the reality of my person, I do so to mislead the consciousness of others (as well as my own). I do so because I feel or believe that who I really am is not acceptable. I value a delusion in someone else's mind above my own knowledge of the truth. The penalty is that I go through life with the tormented sense of being an impostor. This means, among other things, that I sentence myself to the anxiety of wondering *when I will be found out*.

First, I reject myself; that is implicit in living lies, in faking the truth of who I am. Then, I go around feeling rejected by others or looking for possible signs of rejection, which I am typically quick to find. I imagine that the problem is between myself and other people. I do not grasp that the worst of what I fear from others I have already done to myself.

Honesty consists of respecting the difference between the real and the unreal—and of not seeking to gain values by means of faking reality; that is, not seeking to accomplish my goals by pretending that the truth is other than what it is.

When we attempt to live unauthentically, we are always our own first victim, since the fraud is ultimately directed at ourselves.

That the ordinary lies of everyday life are detrimental to self-esteem is obvious—"No, I didn't have a third piece of strawberry shortcake"; "No, I didn't sleep with so-and-so"; "No, I didn't take the money"; "No, I didn't fake the test results"; and so on. The implication is always that the truth is shameful or worse than shameful. That is the message we transmit *to ourselves* when we tell such lies. But this is the obvious level of dishonesty. Here we must consider dishonesty of a much deeper kind, the kind so intimately wedded (so we feel) to our survival that relinquishing it is usually a more formidable challenge.

To avoid a possible misunderstanding, appreciate that living authentically does not mean compulsive truth-telling. It does not mean announcing every possible thought, feeling, or action, regardless of context, appropriateness, or relevance. It does not mean volunteering private truths indiscriminately or promiscuously. It does not mean offering unsolicited opinions about other people's appearance, or offering exhaustive critiques—*necessarily*—even when solicited. It does not mean *volunteering* information about hidden jewels to a burglar.

On the other hand, we must recognize that most of us have been encouraged to be confused about living authentically almost from the day we were born.

Most of us were raised and educated in ways that make an appreciation of authenticity exceedingly difficult. We learned very early to deny what we are feeling, to wear a mask, and ultimately to lose contact with many aspects of our inner selves. We became *unconscious* of much of our inner selves—in the name of adjustment to the world around us.

Our elders encouraged us to disown fear, anger, and pain, because such feelings made them uncomfortable. Often they didn't know how to respond when the pretense of family harmony was shattered. Many of us were also encouraged to hide (and eventually extinguish) our excitement. It got on their nerves. It made our elders unpleasantly aware of what they surrendered long ago. Excitement disrupts routine.

Emotionally remote and inhibited parents tend to raise emotionally remote and inhibited children, not only through their explicit communications, but through their own behavior, which proclaims to the child what is proper, appropriate, and socially acceptable.

Further, since so much in childhood is frightening, bewildering, painful, and frustrating, we learn emotional repression as a defense mechanism, as a way of making life more tolerable. We learn all too quickly how to avoid the nightmare. In order to survive, we learn to "play dead."

"Playing dead" is so common that we generally find it a normal and even desirable state of affairs. It is the familiar, the "comfortable," whereas aliveness can feel strange, even disorienting. And yet "playing dead" is a policy of self-rejection and self-estrangement.

One of the most painful and disorienting experiences of childhood that people are driven to repress is the realization that most adults are liars. This, too, may become a barrier to understanding and valuing authenticity.

I hear Mother lecture me on the virtue of honesty and then I hear her lie to Father. Father announces how much he despises someone and then later proceeds to flatter that person all through dinner. I see a teacher flagrantly deny the truth to another student rather than acknowledge that she, the teacher, made a mistake.

To my knowledge, no psychologist has ever studied the traumatic impact on young people of the magnitude of lying among adults. And yet, when I raise the issue in therapy and invite my clients to explore it, most of them maintain that it was among the most quietly devastating of all early experiences.

Many young people conclude that growing up means learning to accept lying as normal—that is, accepting and embracing unreality as a way of life.

But if we permit ourselves this form of mind-sacrifice, if we allow ourselves to be ruled by fear, if we attach more importance to what other people believe than to what we know to be true—if we value *belonging* above *being*—we will not attain authenticity. To attain it, courage and independence are needed, especially since we encounter these qualities so rarely in others. But this should not deter us; if the people who are authentic are a minority, so are the people who are happy; so are the people who have good self-esteem; so are the people who know how to love.

While the quality of their relationships is clearly superior to that of persons of low self-esteem, high-self-esteem men and women are far from universally liked. Being more independent than the average, they are more outspoken. They are more open about their thoughts and feelings. If they are happy and excited, they are not afraid to show it. If they are suffering, they do not feel obliged to "make nice." If they hold unpopular opinions, they express them nonetheless. They are healthily self-assertive. And because they are not afraid to be who they are—to live authentically—they sometimes arouse the envy and hostility of those more bound by convention.

Sometimes, in their innocence, they are astonished by this response, and sometimes they may feel hurt by it. But they are not led to surrender their own commitment to truth because of it. They do not value the good opinion of others above their own self-esteem. They merely learn that there are people whom it is best to avoid.

They seek out nurturing relationships rather than noxious ones—in contrast to low-self-esteem persons, who seem almost always to end up in noxious relationships.

The relationships of high-self-esteem persons are characterized by higher-than-average degrees of benevolence, respect, and mutually supported dignity. Growth-oriented men and women tend to support the growth aspirations of others. Persons who enjoy their own excitement enjoy the excitement of others. Persons who practice straight talk appreciate straight talk in those they deal with. Persons who feel comfortable saying yes when they want to say yes, and no when they want to say no, respect the right of others to do likewise. Persons who are authentic make the best, most trustworthy friends because others know where they stand with them—and because such persons inspire others to match their authenticity.

In being authentic, we not only honor ourselves—we offer a gift to whomever we deal with.

"Sometimes I give people a false impression of what I feel—" said a client who complained that no one understood her, "when I smile and inside I'm crying; when I try to impress people I don't respect; when I deny my anger and smolder inside; when I pretend that nothing bothers me; when I don't confront anybody about anything; when I appear to agree with whomever is speaking; when I don't say what I want; when I say yes when I want to say no."

"Sometimes I make it hard for people to give me what I want—" said a client who complained that no one cared about his desires, "when I don't tell them what I want; when I pretend I don't want anything; when I act like I'm totally self-sufficient; when I subtly sneer at people's efforts to be good to me; when I criticize everything; when I give and give to other people and use that giving to keep them at a distance; when I act remote; when I won't stand still when people are trying to reach out to me; when I won't even let myself know what I want."

"If I were willing to say no when I want to say no—" said a woman who complained that people took advantage of her, "I'd have more self-respect; I wonder if people would like me; I'd feel cleaner; I would have more time to do the things I want; I wouldn't resent people; I would be kinder; I wouldn't rebel and say no over such petty things; people would know me; I think overall I would be more generous; I couldn't feel like a martyr; I'd be responsible for what happened to me; I couldn't blame anyone; it would all be up to me; I couldn't feel sorry for myself; I'd have dignity."

"If I said yes when I wanted to say yes—" said a man who complained that his life was boring, "I'd have more courage; I'd be taking more risks; I'd have to let people know who I am; I'd have to be honest about the things I care about; I'd reach out to people more often; I'd have adventures; I wouldn't be so self-protective; I wouldn't be so cautious; I'd be a participant in life rather than an observer; more of me would be in reality."

"If I am not here to live up to someone else's expectations—" said a woman overpreoccupied with gaining others' approval, "I'd tell people what I really think and feel; I'd have to find my own direction; I'd have to stand up for myself; I'd have to take responsibility for my own life; I'd find out who my friends really are; maybe I can belong to myself; it's time to ask myself what *I* think is important."

"If I were more honest about my thoughts and opinions—" said a man who complained of social anxiety, "I wonder how people would react; I think I would feel more secure; I know I would feel stronger; I would be more relaxed; I wouldn't feel so intimidated; I'd like myself more; I'd trust myself more; I wouldn't worry so much about other people's opinions; I'd be less anxious; I wouldn't feel like a second-class citizen; I'd know I was a member of the human race."

"If I were more honest about what I feel—" said a woman who complained of having no identity, "I'd have to know what I feel; I think people would have more respect for me; I would have more respect for myself; I'd have to face disapproval sometimes; I would probably lose some friends; I wouldn't always be tiptoeing around other people's feelings; I'd have more integrity; I'd have to change my way of life; I wouldn't say I don't know who I am; I'd feel I have a center; I'd feel there's something to me; I wouldn't feel so empty; I wouldn't feel so phony; it would be scary; I'd be myself; *I'd have a self.*"

In thinking about the issue of living authentically, here are some basic questions to consider. (There is some overlapping among them.)

Am I generally honest with myself about what I am feeling, *accepting* my emotions, *experiencing* them, without necessarily being compelled to act on them?

Am I generally honest with others about my feelings, in contexts where talking about feelings is appropriate?

Do I consciously strive to be truthful and accurate in my communications?

Do I talk comfortably, openly, and straightforwardly about that which I love, admire, and enjoy?

If I am hurt, angry, or upset, do I talk about this with honesty and dignity?

Do I stick up for myself and honor my needs and interests?

Do I allow other people to see my excitement?

If I know I am wrong, do I acknowledge this simply and candidly?

Do I feel that the self I experience internally is the self I present to the world?

Using, once again, a scale from 1 to 10, with 10 representing optimal authenticity and 1 representing the lowest level conceivable, rate yourself on each of these items. Of course, your willingness to be authentic will be challenged in how you rate yourself. Perhaps you will see more clearly the areas in which you are inadequately self-assertive.

Next, take a few minutes to sit quietly alone and meditate on the lies you are presently living. Do so without self-reproach; the purpose of this exercise is not to evoke guilt but to achieve greater clarity and self-understanding, as a prelude to enhanced authenticity of being. Imagine you are telling your story to a loving and compassionate friend who genuinely wants to understand you, wants to know why it feels so necessary or desirable for you to live this particular lie (or lies). Tell your friend what you feel to be the functional utility—the survival value—of your lack of authenticity. Then imagine that your friend invites you to explore your fantasies of what would happen if you gave up living this lie. Spell out in detail what you imagine would happen. Then imagine your friend asking if there are any conditions or circumstances under which you can see yourself being more authentic in this area—and answer. Then, sit quietly and imagine how you might feel, how you might experience yourself, if you chose to live more authentically. Take the time to think this through. Do this exercise for ten minutes once a week for two months . . . and I can virtually guarantee that living more authentically will feel more and more natural, and more and more desirable, and that you will feel less anxious and more self-confident.

You can explore this territory further via sentence completion, writing six to ten endings for each of the following:

The hard thing about being honest with myself about what I'm feeling is—

The hard thing about being honest with others about my feelings is—

If I strived to be true and accurate in my communications—

If I talked openly about the things I love, admire, and enjoy—

If I were honest about feeling hurt, angry, or upset—

If I were willing to show others my excitement—

If I were honest about it when I knew I was wrong—

If I were willing to let people hear the music inside of me—

When I think of what I surrender for fear of being condemned—

When I think of what I surrender for fear of being laughed at—

If I were willing to experiment with being a little more authentic every day—

No one leaps from being relatively unauthentic to being relatively authentic in a moment. That is the significance of the last stem. The question is: Are you willing to discover what happens if, step by step, you experiment with raising the level of your authenticity?

Inside, we do not respect ourselves for our lapses of authenticity. A bad taste is left in the soul. We sense that a betrayal is involved and we are right. But if we are unwilling to confront the issue, we try for a loser's consolation: "I couldn't help it."

Or we say, "It's easy for so-and-so to be honest and straightforward, since he has such good self-esteem. I don't." We forget the fact that living authentically is one of the ways we cultivate self-esteem.

To assert our own wants and needs (without expecting, of course, that anyone else be responsible for their fulfillment), even when it is difficult to do so—this is what our self-esteem asks of us? Yes.

To tell the truth about what we think and feel, without knowing in advance how others will respond? Yes.

To allow others to see and know who we are? Yes.

To remain loyal to our own consciousness, even if we are alone to see what we see and know what we know? Yes.

This is the heroism of honoring the self. It is also the path to high self-esteem.

But wait. Looking back at the distance you have come since you began reading, you may be tempted to protest, "I didn't think I would have to *do* so much!" Perhaps you imagined that all you would be asked to do is utter a few pleasant affirmations every day, and your self-esteem would blossom. That is the kind of attitude that virtually guarantees inadequate self-esteem. "Life," quoting Ayn Rand, "is a process of self-sustaining and self-generated action," and every value pertaining to life requires continuous actions to support and maintain it. You cannot put food in your mouth, or sustain a successful enterprise, merely by uttering affirmations. Neither can you sustain a high level of self-esteem.

If you bought a book entitled *How to Have a Well-Conditioned Body*, you would be realistic enough to know at the outset that action and discipline will be needed. Merely telling yourself, "Every day in every way my body is getting in better and better condition," wouldn't do it. You need the same realism in approaching *How to Raise Your Self-Esteem*.

Just as you will not always be in the mood to work out physically, so you will not always be in the mood to do the exercises in this book. But if you persevere (in either case), two things will become clear: The process gets easier and more appealing, as you get in better "shape"—and when you look in the mirror you will see and like the results.

Chapter 9
Nurturing the Self-Esteem of Others

While each of us is ultimately responsible for his or her self-esteem, we have the option of supporting or assaulting the self-confidence and self-respect of anyone we deal with, just as others have that option in their interactions with us.

Probably all of us can think of occasions when someone dealt with us in a way that acknowledged our dignity as well as his or her own. And we can recall occasions when someone dealt with us as if the concept of human dignity had no reality. We know the difference in how those two kinds of experiences feel.

Turning this example around, probably all of us can think of occasions when we dealt with someone in a spirit of mutual dignity. And we can probably recall occasions when, out of fear or hurt or anger, we dropped to a barely human level of communication, when for the moment dignity lost all meaning for us. And we know the difference in how those two kinds of experiences feel, too.

When our human interactions have dignity we enjoy

them more—and when *we* manifest dignity we like ourselves more.

When we behave in ways that support the self-esteem of others, we support our own.

Let us consider what some of these ways are.

There are certain psychotherapists who are able to have a profound impact on the self-esteem of people who consult them. These psychotherapists may come out of very different theoretical orientations, and utilize very different techniques, and yet in their presence the self-esteem of the client is inspired to rise, as the person discovers new possibilities of functioning that had never seemed real before.

If we understand some of the most important characteristics of how these therapists relate to people, we can apply the principles to our own interactions. There is nothing esoteric about this knowledge. Ideally, it should be available to everyone. My personal dream is that one day it will be taught to schoolchildren.

I (and various graduate students) have questioned clients of mine many times over the years in order to learn which behaviors of mine were experienced as most helpful to the strengthening of the clients' self-esteem. Certain themes recurred again and again. None of them is unique to me. The behaviors I am about to describe will be found among any psychotherapists who know how to facilitate the growth of self-esteem.

To begin with, we treat human beings from the premise of respect. This for me is the first imperative of effective psychotherapy. This is conveyed in how I greet clients when they arrive in the office, how I look at them, how I talk, and how I listen. This entails such matters as courtesy; eye contact; being noncondescending; being nonmoralistic; listening attentively; being concerned with understanding and with being understood; being appropriately spontaneous; refusing to be cast in the role of omniscient authority; refusing to believe the client is incapable of growth. The respect is unrelenting, regardless of the client's behavior. The message is conveyed: A human being is an entity deserving of respect. A client, for whom being treated in this manner may be a rare or even unique experience, may be stimulated over time to begin to restructure his or her self-concept.

I recall a man once saying to me, "Looking back over our therapy, I feel that nothing else that happened was quite so impactful as the simple fact that I always felt respected by you. I pulled everything I could to make you despise me and throw me out. I kept trying to make you act like my father. You refused to cooperate. Somehow, I had to deal with that, I had to let that in, which was difficult at first, but as I did the therapy began to take hold." I remembered that at one of our first sessions he had remarked, "My father would talk to any busboy with more courtesy than he ever showed to me."

When a client is describing feelings of fear, or pain, or anger, it is not helpful to respond with, "Oh, you shouldn't feel that!" A therapist is not a cheerleader. There is great value (for a therapy client or for anyone else) in expressing feelings without having to deal with criticism, condemnation, sarcasm, or lectures. The process of expression is often intrinsically healing. A therapist who is uncomfortable with a client's expression of strong feelings needs to work on him- or herself. To be able to listen serenely and with empathy is basic to the healing arts. It is also basic to authentic friendship, to say nothing of love.

Contrast this with friends who interrupt you with

sermons or advice—or a change of subject—when you attempt to communicate powerful emotions; as if your friends have no confidence in you—or in themselves.

As a therapist, I regard one of my first tasks to be that of creating a context in which the persons who come to me can express their thoughts and opinions without fear of ridicule or reproach. But clearly such a policy should not be confined to psychotherapists. If you agree that you have nothing to gain by making people afraid to speak in your presence, then ask yourself whether you create a context of openness for people when they interact with you.

One of the experiences that people hope for in therapy (and out of therapy) is that of being *visible*—seen and understood. Possibly they have felt alienated and invisible since childhood, and they long for a different sense of themselves. Respecting this desire and understanding its legitimacy, I seek to respond appropriately by sharing observations about the client and providing feedback that allows the client to feel seen and heard. "I think I hear you saying . . ." "I imagine you might be feeling . . ." "Right now you look as if . . ." "Let me tell you how I understand your viewpoint. . . ."

But surely this is *human* communication, not merely psychotherapeutic communication. We *all* long for the experience of visibility and understanding. Should we not seek to give it to one another, to make it a natural part of human encounters?

Effective therapists judge but are not "judgmental." They judge in that they obviously assess some behaviors as superior to others from the point of view of the long-term happiness and well-being of the client. They are not so hypocritical as to pretend that they are without standards—or without likes and dislikes. But they do not moralize and they do not seek to change behavior by evoking guilt. Thus, they do not say, "Only a sick person would do that." Or, "Do you know how immoral you are?" Or, "Until you acknowledge your depravity, I can't help you." Or, "Not very bright, are you?"

When we bombard people with our evaluations of their character, intelligence, and the like, we may intimidate but we do not inspire growth, confidence, or self-respect. And the alternative to being moralistic and "judgmental" is not a policy of bombarding with compliments and extravagant praise. This often intensifies feelings of unworthiness (or invisibility) in the recipient since he or she knows that the speaker is not accurate. We can learn to say what we like or dislike, admire or do not admire, without labeling, assaulting, or praising unrealistically. "I really enjoy you when you . . ." "I am not comfortable when you . . ." "I felt hurt when you . . ." "I felt inspired by your . . ."

In my experience, helpful therapists are compassionate, but they are not sentimental and they do not encourage passivity or self-pity. Any number of my clients have commented on the importance of this distinction for their progress in therapy. I ask, "What do you see as your alternatives?" "What do you think you might do to improve your situation?" "What action are you willing to take?" I do not interrupt with such questions if a person is just beginning to express suffering. But a time usually comes when these questions need to be asked. I believe that part of my job consists of awakening the client to an action orientation.

In dealing with family, friends, and associates there will inevitably be times when we can help them, if we choose to, by conveying just this perspective.

Effective therapists are kind, but they do not let their

clients walk all over them. They do not, for example, self-sacrificially allow clients to call on them at any hour of the day or night over trivial matters. They do not allow themselves to be financially exploited. They require that the value of their time be recognized. They do not leave a client's insulting manners or hostility unconfronted (unless as a specific, *time-limited strategy* for therapeutic purposes). They draw lines. They set limits. So do good parents. So do intelligent friends. So do self-respecting persons in all settings. In taking proper care of themselves, of their own needs and time, therapists *set an example*. They signal: This is how I treat myself and this is how you should treat yourself. Thus, there is no clash between rational selfishness (honorable respect for one's own interests) on one hand and professional responsibility on the other.

This has relevance to all of us. Just as self-sacrificing parents do not set a good example ("I gave up my life for you"), but merely teach their children that it is proper to regard themselves as objects of sacrifice—which tends to generate resentment, hatred, and guilt in the children—so self-sacrificing friends ("My needs don't matter") are a burden, not a joy or an inspiration or an example of anything positive we want to learn.

I am keenly aware that behavior, including the most undesirable behavior, at some level has functional utility, within the knowledge and context of the individual involved. Therefore, I wish to understand the model of self-in-the-world from which the client is operating—as contrasted with merely dismissing the behavior as "crazy." For example, a wife's angry shrieking, which may be very unpleasant to witness, makes its own kind of unhappy sense if we know that nothing less has ever caught her husband's attention, and that she has no sense of an alternative that would work better.

To repeat a point made earlier in the book, we do not understand a person if we merely label him or her as "rotten," "thoughtless," "immoral," and the like. To understand, we need to know the context in which the person's behavior makes some kind of sense or feels desirable or even necessary, even if objectively it is totally irrational.

On the level of our personal relationships, this means helping a person who is behaving inappropriately to identify where he or she is coming from, to grasp what needs are trying to be satisfied—in other words, to bring to that person the understanding and compassion I suggested in an earlier chapter we should bring to ourselves. "What were you feeling at the time?" "What options did you see yourself as having?" "What did you think the person was saying, to whom you were reacting so strongly?" "How did you see the situation?" Obviously we cannot practice this policy equally with every person we encounter. But with people we love or really care about—or perhaps people we work with—it is a powerful tool.

Remember that paralyzing guilt does not serve anyone's interests. And in saying this, there is no implication of glossing over wrongdoing or of sponsoring amoralism. There are obviously times when we need to say, "Your behavior is completely unacceptable to me." Or even, "I don't wish to associate with you." But if our goal is to induce a behavioral change, and an increase in self-esteem to support the change, then in many instances the strategy suggested above has much to recommend it.

One of the characteristics of effective therapists, like the best teachers and coaches, is that they know their clients have greater potential than the clients themselves may recognize. "You don't believe you can master algebra? I believe you can." "You don't think you can jump higher? Try again." "You say you don't dare act against your parents' beliefs? I believe you are capable of thinking for yourself and running your own life." In other words, they do not buy into the person's negative self-concept. This is a point of the highest importance.

A client once remarked to a young psychologist who was studying with me, "If you're asking me what factors I think were most responsible for the success of therapy, I would rank first Nathaniel's conviction that I could do all kinds of things I felt I couldn't do. I didn't think I could ever earn my living at something I really enjoyed. Now I'm doing it. I never could picture myself happily in love. Now I am. I would tell Nathaniel I was hopeless and he would say something like, 'I hear you. Shall we continue?'"

If we wish to nurture the self-esteem of another person, we need to relate to that person from our own vision of his or her worth and value, providing an experience of acceptance and respect. We need to remember that almost all of us tend to underestimate our inner resources—and to keep that thought central in our awareness. We are capable of more than we believe. If we remain clear about this, others can acquire this knowledge from us almost by contagion.

We can learn, for example, to listen to a person's expression of feelings even when those feelings are self-doubt and insecurity. And we can listen without indulging any impulse to lecture or debate, because we understand that fully owning and experiencing unwanted feelings is the first step toward transcending them.

Of course we must recognize that sometimes a person

may use self-disparaging remarks to manipulate us into disagreeing and paying compliments. We can refuse to participate in that game, by saying, "I wonder what the pay-off is for putting yourself down right now."

It can be very difficult to go on believing in another person when that person seems not to believe in him- or herself. And yet one of the greatest gifts we can offer is our refusal to accept a person's poor self-concept at face value, seeing through it to the deeper, stronger self that exists within if only as a potential. We cannot always succeed. We can only try. Optimally, we will bring out the best within the other person. At minimum, we will strengthen the best in ourselves.

Finally, to whatever extent we are rational, congruent, and consistent in our dealings with people, we present them with an intelligible and comprehensible impression of reality—and any competent psychotherapist, and any self-respecting human being, strives to offer this sanity in his or her interactions. Thus, we signal: Your mind is competent to deal with me; I am not presenting a bewildering and contradictory impression of reality such as would leave you feeling confused, impotent, and powerless. And when we are rational, congruent, and consistent, of course our own self-esteem benefits.

These observations are relevant equally to our dealings with adults and with children. Since I explore the subject of child-parent relationships in *Honoring the Self*, I shall not cover that ground again here. What I am sketching now are general guidelines applicable to *all* our relationships.

But if you have children, go over the preceding descriptions of behaviors and consider how consistently you practice them—because children need these behaviors from you even more than adults do.

"If I had had the experience of being respected as a child"; "If someone had believed in me when I was young"; "If someone had conveyed that my wants and feelings mattered"; "If someone had seen me as a unique individual"—I have heard countless clients in therapy say to me, in sentence-completion exercises—"I would have learned self-respect; I might believe in myself; I would take my own wants seriously and work to fulfill them; I would have a clearer sense of who I am."

The more we work on ourselves, the more we seem to acquire greater appropriateness in our interactions. No parent of healthy self-esteem is likely to think that ridiculing a child will inspire competence and independence. No teacher of good self-esteem will need to be told that sarcasm is not a good teaching tool. No self-respecting executive is likely to think he will elicit the best from people by treating them with contempt. No self-confident human being tries to keep friends by posing as an authority and manipulating them through their insecurities.

In the area of child-parent relationships it is clear that, while nothing is guaranteed, the best way to inspire good self-esteem in children is to possess it ourselves (just as the best way to inspire sane sexual attitudes is to have them ourselves). But the principle is wider. If we wish to make a positive contribution to the self-concept of others—*any* others, not just children—then self-esteem (like charity) begins at home, with ourselves.

Serenity inspires serenity, happiness inspires happiness, openness inspires openness, and when we live from the best within ourselves we are most likely to draw out the best in others.

If we have the courage to let others see our excitement, we imply that excitement is a value and that they should not suppress their own. If we let others see our passion for our goals, we implicitly bestow our sanction on their own capacity for passionate goal-seeking. If we proudly honor our own values and interests, we signal others that they have a right to honor theirs. If we have the integrity to be who we are, we may inspire that integrity in others.

And so, in honoring the self, we help build a community of persons with healthy self-esteem. Individualism is not the adversary of community but its most vital pillar.

If these ideas seem valid to you, what do they mean in terms of your interactions with people during the next month of your life? And the month after that?

Chapter 10
The Question of Selfishness

Self-esteem is often confused with spurious notions of "selfishness."

While the cultural trend to which I am referring is in evidence everywhere, I encountered this misunderstanding personally while on a promotional tour for *Honoring the Self*. There is currently an unthinking tendency to dismiss as "narcissistic" any individual actively concerned with his or her personal development, a kind of backlash against the human-potential movement. "Self," it appears, has become an inflammatory word, at least in some circles.

Self-esteem, self-actualization, self-realization—even the quest for autonomy—are becoming morally suspect. "Haven't we had enough of the 'me generation'?" interviewers kept asking. "Aren't you encouraging selfishness?"

While I was personally treated warmly, I could not help but notice the disquietude that the mere words *honoring the self* seemed to evoke. "What about the problems of the world?" they said. "Aren't you interested in going beyond the isolated individual? What about relationships?" And, "Don't most people have too big an ego already?"

Since these questions are asked so often, it is reasonable to assume that they disclose something about the assumptions of a great many people. It is these assumptions we need to challenge.

Let me mention that neither in *Honoring the Self* nor in any of my previous work has my message been, "Me first—with no regard for the rights of others." Rather, I have been concerned with exploring the relationship between self-esteem and human well-being, individually and socially. In the course of this pursuit I have seen clearly that the values of individualism and enlightened self-interest provide the best possible basis for social cooperation, benevolence, and progress.

Ask yourself with whom you would like to share the world. People who respect your right to exist and do not ask you to act against your own self-interest—or people who treat you as an object of sacrifice? People who enjoy a strong sense of personal identity—or those who expect you to create one for them? People who take responsibility for their own existence—or those who attempt to pass that responsibility to you? These are, of course, some of the *social* consequences of both high and low self-esteem.

It is easy enough to point to some narcissists who talk about "pursuing my personal growth" or "pursuing my self-esteem." It is easy because narcissism can be found anywhere. But individualism, self-esteem, autonomy, a concern with personal development—these traits are not narcissistic. Narcissism is a condition of unhealthy and excessive self-absorption that arises from a deep-rooted sense of inner deficiency and deprivation. Ironically, the vices typically ascribed to persons with strong egos—

pettiness, belligerent competitiveness, overreadiness to take offense—are, in fact, the afflictions peculiar to weak egos.

I cannot imagine any rational person suggesting that self-actualization—that is, the realization of our positive potentials—is to be pursued without involvement in and commitment to personal relationships. "Isn't it to my self-interest," I asked my interviewers, "to find people I can love, respect, and admire?" I would usually see a light bulb go on in their answering smiles. "Isn't it to my self-interest to live in a safer, saner, better world—and to try to bring such a world about?"

The polarization of self and others, or self and the world, has no valid basis in reality. Indeed, there is overwhelming evidence that the higher the level of an individual's self-esteem, the more likely that he or she will treat others with respect, kindness, and generosity. People who do not experience self-love have little or no capacity to love others. People who experience deep insecurities and self-doubts tend to experience other human beings as frightening and inimical. People who have little or no self-esteem have nothing to contribute to the world.

In light of all this we must ask: Why do the concepts of self-esteem and self-actualization—that is, personal goals—strike some people as so ominous? Why are only "social" goals respectable?

The answer, I believe, lies in the failure of many people to free themselves from an authoritarian notion of ethics which places its concepts of the good outside of the individual, which means *outside of you*. We encounter this viewpoint in many different ways in families, schools, churches, and certainly in government.

In fact, almost all ethical systems that have achieved some measure of world influence have been variations on the theme of self-surrender and self-sacrifice. While unselfishness is equated with virtue, selfishness is made a synonym of evil. In these systems, the individual always becomes the victim, twisted against him- or herself and commanded to be "unselfish" in service to some allegedly higher value—pharaoh, emperor, king, the tribe, the country, the family, the true faith, the race, the state, the proletariat, or society (or "the planet").

We would more readily understand the willingness of so many persons to submit themselves to one kind of authority figure or another, under whose rule atrocities are sometimes committed, if we remembered how almost all of us were introduced to the word *good*. "He's a good boy—he minds me, he behaves." "She's a good girl—she does what she's told." From the beginning we are instructed that virtue consists not of honoring the needs, wants, and highest possibilities of the self, but rather of satisfying the expectations of others. "Living for others" is construed as the essence of morality, and those who preach it are more interested in obedience than in self-esteem. As a psychologist, I cannot remember a time when I did not perceive this doctrine as disastrous for mental and emotional well-being.

Today, with the rise of feminism, women are beginning to awaken to the fact that this doctrine is manipulative and exploitive. Imagine the response if a lecturer told a group of modern women, "Don't think of your own needs and wants—think only of the needs and wants of those you serve. Self-sacrifice is the highest virtue." Men, too, need to take a fresh look at this doctrine as it affects their lives. It is no respecter of gender. The issue is global.

The misfortune is that many men and women struggling with issues of self-realization feel helpless and intimidated by accusations of selfishness. Well, if "selfishness" means "concerned with one's self-interest," *of course* the pursuit of self-esteem and personal development is selfish. So is the pursuit of physical health. So is the pursuit of sanity. So is the pursuit of happiness. So is the pursuit of your next breath of air.

If this is evil, *how are we to exist?* We cannot repudiate self without repudiating life.

In order to live successfully, then, we need an ethic of rational self-interest. Until we are prepared to respect an individual's right to his or her own life—until we understand that every person, ourselves included, is an end in him- or herself, not a means to the ends of others—we cannot think clearly about our own existence or the requirements of human happiness.

Until we are willing to honor the self and proudly proclaim our right to do so, we cannot fight for self-esteem—and we cannot achieve it.

Chapter 11
Summary: The Impact of Self-Esteem

How do we grow in self-esteem? Let us summarize some key points.

• We must remember that self-esteem is not determined by worldly success, physical appearance, popularity, or any other value not directly under our volitional control. Rather, it is a function of our rationality, honesty, and integrity, all volitional processes, all operations of mind for which we are responsible.

Here is a sentence-completion exercise that will help bring into focus where you stand on this issue at present. Indeed, this exercise and the ones that follow will tell you a good deal about what you have absorbed from the book thus far—and may point the way to where further work needs to be done.

If I look at the criteria by which I judge myself— If no one can give me good self-esteem except myself—

If I choose to understand what self-esteem depends on—
One of the things I can do to raise my self-esteem is—

• Since positve self-esteem is the feeling, experience, and conviction of being appropriate to life and to the challenges of life, and since our mind is our basic tool of survival, the central pillar of healthy self-esteem is a policy of living consciously (which *entails* rationality, honesty, and integrity). Living consciously is living responsibly toward reality, living with a respect for facts, knowledge, and truth—and a policy of *generating a level of awareness appropriate to our actions.*

If I allow myself to understand the meaning of living consciously—
If I am not yet fully ready to live consciously—
If I were willing to know what I'm doing when I act—
If I were willing to see what I see and know what I know—

• Self-acceptance is a refusal to deny or disown any aspect of the self: our thoughts, emotions, memories, physical attributes, subpersonalities, or actions. Self-acceptance is the refusal to be in an adversarial relationship to our own experience. It is the foundation of all growth and change. It is the courage, in the ultimate sense, to be *for* ourselves. The level of our self-esteem cannot be higher than the level of our self-acceptance.

As I learn to accept myself—
One of the things I need to learn to accept is—

As I give up fighting myself—
As I breathe into my feelings rather than resist
them—
As I learn to own my actions—
I am becoming aware—

• If we are to protect our self-esteem, we need to know how to assess appropriately our own behavior. This includes, first, being certain that the standards by which we judge are truly our own, and not merely values of others to which we feel obliged to pay lip service. Second, we need to bring to our assessments an attitude not only of honesty but also of compassion—a willingness to consider the context and circumstances of our actions, as well as the options or alternatives we perceive as available to us. In matters where we feel truly and appropriately guilty, we need to take *specific steps* to resolve the guilt rather than merely suffer passively.

If it turns out that living with guilt is a cop-out—
If I were willing to forgive myself—
As I seek to understand why I act as I do—
As I learn to live by my own standards—

• We must learn *never* to apologize for, reproach ourselves for, or try to disown our virtues. We must have the courage of our strengths and assets. Otherwise, inevitably we betray self-esteem.

If I refuse to apologize for my virtues—
If I am honest about my assets—
If I take pleasure in myself—
If I admit that I like myself—

• We need to recognize, befriend, dialogue with, and ultimately embrace our subselves or subpersonalities, so that we can feel whole, undivided, *integrated*.

**As I learn to embrace my child-self—
As I learn to embrace my teenage-self—
If I disown the person I once was—
If I make friends with all the parts of me—
I am beginning to see that—**

• We need to live actively rather than passively, to take responsibility for our choices, feelings, actions, and well-being—to take responsibility for the fulfillment of our own desires—to take responsibility for our own existence. Like independence, productiveness is a basic self-esteem virtue, work being one of the practical forms of manifesting self-responsibility.

**If I take full responsibility for my actions—
If I take full responsibility for the things I say—
If I persist in blaming other people—
If I insist on seeing myself as a victim—
If I accept that my happiness is mine alone to achieve—**

• Self-confidence and self-respect are sustained by living authentically. This is the courage to be who we are, to preserve congruence between our inner self and the self we present to the world. In the literal sense, this means living self-assertively; that which we think, value, and feel, we manifest in the world. We do not consign ourselves to the underground of the unexpressed and unlived.

As I learn to be more honest about what I think and feel—
As I learn to be honest about my wants—
When I think about some of the lies I have lived by—
When I am ready to give those lies up—
If I need time to learn to live with integrity—
If I were willing to give myself the time I need to learn—
If I were willing to let people hear the music inside of me—
If I were willing to show people who I am—
As I learn to simply be myself—

• In supporting the self-esteem of others, we support our own. Thus, self-esteem is served by living benevolently.

If I deal with other people with respect and benevolence—
If I give others the goodwill I want them to give me—
If I allow myself to understand what I have been reading—
If I accept that I may not yet be ready to let all this knowledge in—
If I give myself permission to grow at my own speed—
If this is the beginning of a great adventure—

• We need to understand that, as an ethical-psychological ideal, self-esteem implies and presupposes the supreme value of an individual life. It rests on a moral vision that sees each person as an end in him- or herself, and—opposing the doctrine of self-surrender and self-sacrifice—upholds rational self-interest as a guiding principle.

> If I do not exist to serve other people—
> If other people do not exist to serve me—
> If my life belongs to me—
> If I really do have a right to exist—
> If self-sacrifice won't buy me self-esteem—
> If it takes courage to be honorably selfish—
> I am becoming aware—

Early in the book we saw that each of the behaviors I have summarized above is both a source of good self-esteem and a manifestation of good self-esteem—a cause and a consequence— the principle of reciprocal causation.

How can we raise our self-esteem? By practicing these behaviors. By living consciously, self-acceptingly, responsibly, authentically, benevolently, and with integrity.

There are great rewards in doing so, but there are also challenges. Whatever your present level of self-esteem, and the life you have created to reflect it, right now you may be experiencing the comfort of the familiar—the comfort of the known—and intuitively you may sense that to grow in self-esteem is to leave that comfort zone and enter the unknown.

"If I raise my self-esteem," clients say to me, "how do I know how things will seem to me? Will I still love my spouse? Will my job still be bearable? Will my interests change? Will friends resent me? Will I be lonely?

"I might not always like how I feel," they say, "but it's familiar. I'm used to it, even the bouts with anxiety and depression. I'm in control, in a way. But with significantly higher self-esteem, I wouldn't know myself. Would I feel safe?"

* * *

As you do the exercises in this book, and then practice in your life the behaviors to which the exercises and the discussion point, you will experience an increase in self-confidence and self-respect, but you may also experience some sense of disorientation. In the transition from an old self-concept to a new one—even an improved and happier one—there is often some anxiety. If you persevere in your new learnings and behaviors, and do not fall back into old patterns, you will soon become comfortable with your new sense of self and the anxiety will vanish.

Now, this process applies to self-esteem in general and also to any of the specific practices that enhance self-esteem. For example, as we learn to live more consciously, or more self-acceptingly, we can both enjoy the experience and find it strange—as if we are living in our body with a person we are not sure we know. To be able to accept some disorientation as an inevitable aspect of growth, and to be willing to tolerate it until we arrive at a new sense of the "normal," is essential to successful change.

Perhaps the most eloquent statement of this problem was made by a therapy client many years ago: "Nathaniel, I haven't felt anxious for a week *and it's making me nervous.*"

I have seen clients practice the kind of procedures I present in this book, lose all or much of their depression, then literally fling themselves back into self-torture because they are still attached to an outmoded self-concept that lags behind their actual experience. For years they have seen themselves as sufferers. Their lives were organized around this self-concept, including their relationships. "What is my life about if I am not suffering?" I have heard them say. "If I am not unhappy, how will I act with people? What will I say or do? I have no experience at being happy! Besides, if I'm not happy, I can't lose it, it can't be taken away, whereas if I am happy . . ."

This is an example of the "unknown" of which I spoke a moment ago—the unfamiliar territory into which we step as we rise in self-esteem.

And there is still more—the responses of other people as they witness our changes. If we are more self-assured than we were before, if we convey greater self-respect—or if we are more open, spontaneous, undefensive, or cheerful—then other people's ways of dealing with us may no longer fit, may no longer be appropriate to who we are, and then *they* may become disoriented. Either they will adjust their behaviors to match the new self-concept we project, or (wittingly or unwittingly) they will try to maneuver us back into our old self-concept. Either way, life will not be as it was before. Once again, we confront the unfamiliar, the unknown.

Our resistance to these changes may make us reluctant to participate in the exercises or practice the behaviors described in earlier chapters. We need to combat both inertia and fear. What are the rewards if we accept these feelings and yet do not yield to them—but instead maintain our determination to advance in self-confidence, self-respect, and the enjoyment of life?

On the level of direct, internal experience, the answer by now is clear: greater self-trust and self-love, greater joy in our own being, greater pride in what we have achieved in our own person.

Beyond that, as you grow in self-esteem:

• Your face, manner, and way of talking and moving will tend naturally to project the pleasure you take in being alive.

• At some point you will notice that you are more able to speak of your accomplishments or shortcomings with directness and honesty, since you will be in friendly relationship to facts.

• You will probably find that you are more comfortable in giving and receiving compliments, expressions of affection, appreciation, and the like.

• You will tend to be open to criticism and comfortable about acknowledging mistakes, because your self-esteem is not tied to an image of "perfection."

• Your words and movements will tend to have a quality of ease and spontaneity, since you are not at war with yourself.

• There will increasingly be harmony between what you say and do and how you look, sound, and move.

• You will find that more and more you have an attitude of openness to and curiosity about new ideas, new experiences, new possibilities of life, since for you existence has become an adventure.

• Feelings of anxiety or insecurity, if they present themselves, will be less likely to intimidate or overwhelm you, since managing them and rising above them will seem far easier.

• You will most likely find that you enjoy the humorous aspects of life, in yourself and in others.

• You will be more flexible in responding to situations and challenges, moved by a spirit of inventiveness and even playfulness, since you trust your mind and do not see life as doom or defeat.

• You will be more comfortable with assertive (not belligerent) behavior—you will be quicker to stick up and speak up for yourself.

• You will tend to preserve a quality of harmony and

dignity under conditions of stress, as feeling centered becomes more and more natural to you.

Will you undergo some changes in values in terms of people, work, and recreational activities? Almost inevitably. Will you still know times of conflict, crisis, tough decision-making? Of course—they are intrinsic to life. Will you experience yourself as having far greater resources with which to respond to such challenges? A resounding *yes*.

Even on the physical level, there may be noticeable changes as you grow in self-confidence and self-respect:

- Your eyes may well become more alert, bright, and lively.
- Your face will at some point become more relaxed and (barring illness) will tend to exhibit natural color and good skin vibrancy.
- Your chin will probably be held more naturally and more in alignment with your body.
- Your jaw will tend to become more relaxed.
- Your shoulders typically will become more relaxed yet erect.
- Your hands will tend to be relaxed, graceful, and quiet.
- Your arms will tend to hang in a relaxed, natural way.
- Your posture will tend to be relaxed, erect, well balanced.
- Your walk will tend to be purposeful (without being aggressive and overbearing).
- Your voice will tend to be modulated with an intensity appropriate to the situation, and with clear pronunciation.

* * *

The likelihood is that you will exhibit these traits increasingly, as any number of observers have noted the presence of these physical traits, as well as the psychological traits listed above, in men and women who enjoy healthy self-esteem.

You will notice that the theme of relaxation occurs again and again. Relaxation implies that you are not hiding from yourself and are not at war with who you are, whereas chronic tension conveys a message of some form of internal split, some form of self-avoidance or self-repudiation, some aspect of the self being disowned or held on a very tight leash.

If the psychological and physical traits I have mentioned were to become a natural part of you, ask yourself what difference it would make in your experience of being alive. Ask yourself how you would be affected in your ability to love and be loved. Ask yourself how you would be affected in your approach to work, in the level of your ambition, in the goals you might aspire to reach.

An increase in self-esteem makes a difference. When you are clear on the difference it makes, you will know that the quest is worth it.

And in committing yourself to the journey, you discover that the journey has already begun.

Appendix
Recommendations for Further Study

If reading this book is your first introduction to the subject of self-esteem, I hope you will choose to pursue it further.

You may have already gathered that my most comprehensive discussion of self-esteem is *Honoring the Self.* This book sums up my nearly three decades of work in the field. It is the logical book to read after (or before) *How to Raise Your Self-Esteem.*

For an examination of my theoretical starting point, with particular emphasis on philosophical foundations, I refer you to my earlier book, *The Psychology of Self-Esteem.*

For an exploration of the childhood origins of negative self-concepts, by means of stories taken from my clinical practice, see *Breaking Free.*

For the problem of self-alienation and a discussion of the relation of reason and emotion, see *The Disowned Self.*

For my views regarding love and man/woman relationships, see *The Psychology of Romantic Love* and the revised and expanded edition of *What Love Asks of Us* (formerly titled *The Romantic Love Question & Answer Book* written with Devers Branden).

"If You Could Hear What I Cannot Say" is a workbook that teaches the reader how to use my sentence-completion technique to resolve problems in the area of intimate relationships. *To See What I See and Know What I Know* is a workbook that teaches the use of sentence completion for self-understanding, self-discovery, and self-healing.

All these works are published by Bantam Books.

In addition, I have been developing a series of self-actualization audiocassettes aimed specifically at carrying forward in new ways the material presented in *How to Raise Your Self-Esteem*. You may obtain information about these cassettes, as well as about other, related matters—lectures, seminars, workshops, and the like—by writing to The Biocentric Institute, P.O. Box 2609, Beverly Hills, CA 90213.

ABOUT THE AUTHOR

Author of THE PSYCHOLOGY OF SELF-ESTEEM, BREAKING FREE, THE DISOWNED SELF, THE PSYCHOLOGY OF ROMANTIC LOVE, WHAT LOVE ASKS OF US (with Devers Branden), IF YOU COULD HEAR WHAT I CANNOT SAY, HONORING THE SELF, TO SEE WHAT I SEE AND KNOW WHAT I KNOW, and HOW TO RAISE YOUR SELF-ESTEEM, Nathaniel Branden is a pioneer in his studies of self-esteem, personal transformation, and man/woman relationships.

Dr. Branden is in private practice in Los Angeles and lives in Lake Arrowhead, California.

His works have been published in French, German, Portuguese, Dutch, Hebrew, Greek, Japanese, Swedish, and Italian.

As director of the Biocentric Institute in Los Angeles, he offers Intensive Workshops throughout the United States in self-esteem and man/woman relationships. He also conducts professional training workshops for mental health professionals in his approach to personal growth and development.

Communications to Dr. Branden or requests for information about his various lectures, seminars, and Intensive Workshops should be addressed to The Biocentric Institute, P.O. Box 2609, Beverly Hills, CA 90213-2609.